# directions

## new

FOR
CHILD
DEVELOPMENT

number 1 • 1978

# new
# directions
# for
# child
# development

a quarterly sourcebook
William Damon, Editor-in-Chief

*number 1, 1978*

# social cognition

william damon
editor

Jossey-Bass Inc., Publishers
San Francisco • Washington • London

SOCIAL COGNITION
*New Directions for Child Development*
Number 1, 1978
    William Damon, Editor

*New Directions for Child Development* is published quarterly
by Jossey-Bass, Inc., Publishers. Subscriptions are available
at the regular rate for institutions, libraries, and agencies
of $25 for one year. Individuals may subscribe at the special
professional rate of $15 for one year. Application to mail a
second-class postage rates is pending at San Francisco, California,
and at additional mailing offices.

*Correspondence:*
Subscriptions, single-issue orders, change of address notices,
undelivered copies, and other correspondence should be sent to
*New Directions* Subscriptions, Jossey-Bass, Inc., Publishers,
433 California Street, San Francisco, California 94104.
Editorial correspondence should be sent to the Editor-in-Chief,
William Damon, Department of Psychology,
Clark University, Worcester Massachusetts, 01610.

Library of Congress Catalogue Card Number LC 78-061126

Cover design by Willi Baum

Manufactured in the United States of America

# contents

# editor's notes

Trends in psychology are often shaped by a peculiar convergence of historical and scientific movements. The explosion of research on children's cognitive development in the mid-1950s probably had as much to do with Sputnik and our awakened national concern for science education as with the American rediscovery of Piaget and the consequent decline of behaviorism. In retrospect, such trends seem historically destined, perhaps inevitable.

Suddenly, and increasingly over the last few years, children's social cognition has become a focus of interest in developmental, experimental, and social psychology. Although the term *social cognition* has generally referred to thinking about any social relation, social object, social institution, or social event, research on children's social cognition has flourished particularly in certain areas. Foremost of these areas have been: the child's conception of others ("person perception"), the child's ability to take the perspective of another ("role taking"), the child's understanding of psychological causality ("intentionality"), and the child's moral judgment. Most recently, as indicated by the present volume, developmental psychologists have begun examining the child's conception of interpersonal relations (like friendship), of the self, of nonmoral social regulation, and of social institutions (like government, voting, and money).

As for historical inevitability, one can point to a number of converging trends within and beyond psychology to explain the recent surge of interest in children's social cognition. Within the discipline, many developmental psychologists during the past decade have sensed a gap in child study left by socialization theorists and Piagetian research. As Youniss and Volpe point out in their paper, social-cognitive research has challenged the sociological determinism suggested by socialization theory. Viewing social experiences as occasions in which the child engages in independent thinking, they write that research on children's social cognition has been able to "free the child from being a mere reflection of social input from others." In many ways, Piagetian theory has always shared this constructivist approach, but the preponderance of Piaget-inspired research in the past forty years has focused on children's logical and physical conceptions. Thus, even from a Piagetian perspective, an acknowledged dearth of information exists concerning children's social conceptions. As Furth writes in his chapter, there is a special irony about this dearth, not only because most child psychologists recognize the primary importance of social development, but also because Piaget's theory is as well equipped to deal with social reasoning as with logical reasoning.

In addition to these converging trends in the socialization and Piagetian approaches, a variety of historical influences during the past decade have contributed to the emergence of children's social cognition as a major area of study. Watergate and other recent political scandals spotlighted the evident political and moral immaturity of otherwise well-educated persons: Citizens questioned the adequacy of social and moral development in our culture, just as they had scrutinized scientific development during the Sputnik era. The woman's movement brought attention to sex-role stereotypes and other forms of sex-related social knowledge that children in our society acquire. Children's racial conceptions, another aspect of social knowledge, have also emerged as a subject of concern for a society fearing irreversible schisms. Responding to this social climate, educators have attempted to use their classrooms to help children develop a better understanding of social, political, sexual, and moral issues. However, these instructors have been stymied by the dearth of psychological information on children's social cognition.

It is my belief that the research represented in this sourcebook, in addition to other recent efforts described in David Forbes' literature review, offers us a bright hope of overcoming our ignorance in this area. Without exception, each of the five contributions signals a new theoretical and empirical direction that is bound to generate further investigation and future knowledge about how children come to understand the social world.

Not surprisingly, certain themes run throughout this sourcebook. In some cases, the themes reflect common assumptions, similar methodological approaches, or concomitant research findings; in other cases, they reflect disagreement and dispute. Perhaps the most basic theme concerns the relation between the child's social cognition and the child's intellectual development in general. Furth and Broughton, each from his own perspective, maintain that the distinction between social and logical-physical cognition is a false dualism. Social thinking, argues Furth, becomes quite logical with development; and both Broughton and Furth argue that logical thinking is at its core social, originating as it does from the realm of social discourse. In contrast to Furth and Broughton, Turiel points to certain basic differences between conceptual domains. A child's experience with the physical world differs in many ways from the child's experiences with the social world; consequently, children must organize their thinking differently in each case ("concepts are organized *within* domains and not necessarily *across* domains"). By the same reasoning, Turiel maintains that children's social experience itself has several distinguishable aspects, and he bases his model of social cognition on such distinctions within the social domain. It should be pointed out that Turiel argues this issue on a different level than do Broughton or Furth. The latter two emphasize that all aspects of human knowledge are similar in origin, development, and function; whereas Turiel, focusing on the actual structure of various knowledge components, shows that different concepts are indeed organized differently, as they must be if humans are adequately to know reality in all its variety.

Indeed, in singling out one or another slice of children's social cognition to investigate, all contributors to this volume have implicitly recognized the organizational uniqueness of different social concepts. Each contributor, of course, makes this recognition in his or her own way. Youniss and Volpe make a particularly strong case for the special status of friendship concepts in the lives and social-emotional development of young children. Cooney and Selman conduct their investigation according to a carefully constructed model of interpersonal awareness that systematically distinguishes various issues within the social domain. Broughton and Furth, too, are selective in what they choose to study. The only real difference here lies in the attitudes of the investigators toward dividing the social domain for study. Cooney and Selman's intriguing quotation that "there may be as many ways to map social cognition as there are map makers" indicates their belief that conceptual distinctions in developmental research may be made according to pragmatic goals (in their case, "our special focus reflects our clinical interest"). Taken to its extreme, this reasoning would lead to the view that the conceptual distinctions themselves are somewhat arbitrary when removed from their social purpose; and, although Cooney and Selman would not accept this extreme position, many researchers in the field do. Other authors in this volume explicitly disagree. For Youniss and Volpe, there is a special developmental significance in children's friendship. Broughton's social-cognition categories derive from a weighty philosophical tradition and are hardly arbitrary. For Turiel, a major goal of the investigation itself is to validate a social-conceptual distinction between the moral and the conventional, and he believes that this distinction originates directly in the different types of social interaction (moral versus social order) experienced by children. Again, this is not the stuff of arbitrary conceptual distinctions.

There are a number of other lively disputes that we could cull from this assortment of readings. As one final example, the contributors vary widely in their definitions of "role taking" despite their unanimity concerning the importance of this construct. For Cooney and Selman, role taking is "the basic structure underlying the child's developing (social) understanding," and much of the literature cited in Forbes' review shares this notion. For Turiel, however, role taking is not a structure at all but a method for obtaining information about the social environment. Youniss and Volpe, somewhat like Turiel, consider role taking to be an interpersonal process with somewhat questionable developmental status. From their relational point of view, Youniss and Volpe dispute the common view that the child's major social-developmental accomplishment is to adopt other points of view successfully (generally believed to occur during middle childhood). Rather, they assert that, at least in the case of peer relations, the perspectives of self and other are coconstructed by self and other *from the start*. Consequently, children's social development may best be described as a gradual transforming into principles and social practice the mutuality experienced by the child early in the peer relation, and not as a fundamental structural-developmental transformation in children's role-taking ability. This debate over the nature of role taking is at the heart of social-cognitive study, and its resolution will shape our future theories.

Beyond the themes and contentions that permeate this volume, one general characteristic unifies all the efforts included here. This is the attempt to describe qualitatively children's developing social conceptions. It is in the authors' carefully articulated descriptions of developmental changes, stages, and levels, profusely illustrated by children's quotations and descriptions of other behavior by children, that the real message of this volume is to be found. Here we may find our richest view of children's social cognition, and here we must look for an understanding of the factors that lead to social-cognitive growth. With regard to this last point — understanding the process of development itself — it is Furth's paper that most extensively explores the dymanic and "expanding nature of early developmental stages." In his analysis of the "developmental experiences" to which children's often playful and conflict-filled thinking leads, Furth is able to describe developmental stages as relatively stable modes of knowing the world, and also to demonstrate how stages contain the germs of their own subsequent reorganizations. I know of no finer discussion of the growth-seeking potential of developmental structures. In fact—and here is another historical inevitability in the making—if structural analyses of children's behavior are to have a future, this future must lie in spelling out the developmental processes implicit in developmental stages. Too often children's stages have been presented as static and self-contained patterns of behavior. The time is ripe for attempts like Furth's to capture the movement that, as we all know, is most truly characteristic of the always changing child.

William Damon
Editor

*William Damon is associate professor of psychology at Clark University, Worcester, Massachusetts.*

*Child-child and child-adult relations are not simply*
*different: They may be the sources of two types*
*of social understanding, each serving*
*a distinct developmental function.*

# a relational analysis of
# children's friendship

## james youniss
## jacqueline volpe

Relational theory is an approach in which the development of the self is taken to be simultaneous with the development of understanding of interpersonal relations. This approach is found in Sullivan (1953), who proposes that interpersonal relation is the basic unit of analysis for social science (pp. 16-20). As Sullivan puts it: "I shall . . . begin to trace the developmental history of personality, which as you will see is actually the developmental history of possibilities of interpersonal relations" (p. 30). The same approach is found in Piaget (1932): There are no such things as "isolated individuals. There are only relations" (p. 360); there is no self without the other (p. 318), and the self is a product of relations (p. 393).

For the past four years we have been working toward a theoreti-

Several people have collaborated in developing the ideas and collecting the data presented in this paper. Among them are Gail Cabral, Barbara Gellert, Roger Locker, Michelle Eban, and Peggy Schatzow.

cal statement about social development that embodies the principles of relationship, is grounded in a relational epistemology, and accounts for a determining sociological context. Preliminary approximations appear in Youniss (1975, 1977, forthcoming, in press). The present paper moves one step further and contains some empirical findings that illustrate the theory. The search for an epistemology compatible with the principle of relation forced us away from some traditional views. For many cognitive theorists, the individual "knowing" self is a master of *creating* links with other persons. For example, with maturity, the self comes to figure out what other selves are thinking or feeling and comes to place itself into their perspectives. From this relational point of view, the task of the self is to make these achievements as it develops cognitively.

While role taking and similar processes are obviously important to social functioning, they imply a model of cognition that is not helpful to relational theory. In our view of relation, there is *always* some mutuality between the thought of self and other. By this we mean that the self has insight into the meanings that another person will give to social interaction. If self and other did not share meanings, they could hardly interact sensibly, such as when they seek either individual or common goals.

The identification of cognition with an individualistic view of thinking is deep-seated in psychological theory and may be legitimately granted the status of an ideology (Sampson, 1977). It will not do, however, for a relational approach, which needs an individual thinker who from the start contructs thought with, rather than independently from, other persons. This is why we have turned to Piaget's (1932) epistemology, which offers ideas like the following: Rationality in thought "appears as the fruit of a mutual engagement. And what is this rational rule but the primitive motor rule freed from individual caprice and submitted to the control of reciprocity?" (p. 88), and "The individual as such knows only anomie. . . . Autonomy therefore appears only with reciprocity" (p. 196).

For Piaget, social understanding begins with interpersonal interaction, in which persons compare, contrast, and confront one another with their own thinking (p. 393). The thought that each takes away is not a private construct but the result of a collaborative operation. Without collaboration, thought is subjective, egocentric, and alienating (p. 36). Indeed, it is hard to see what, if anything, is social in thought that has been privately constructed.

For decades developmental psychologists assumed that sociological factors should be seen as determining influences on social development. This assumption meshed with the philosophy of classical empiricism as it was interpreted for behavioristic learning theories. The widespread strength of this view can be found in compendiums like Goslin (1969), where several of its specific versions are reported.

The "new look" in social development, called *social cognition,* began to appear in the 1960s. One of its aims was to counter the sociological-determination viewpoint. Theorists wanted to free the child from being a mere reflection of social input from others. They therefore stressed that social experiences were occasions for thinking. The child who had these experiences was able to participate in them but was still able to construct a somewhat independent view of "social reality" (compare Shantz, 1975).

The immediate result of this introduction of cognition was a challenge from traditional socialization theorists. There was much debate, but eventually cognition in some form entered socialization theories, such as that of Bandura (1969). Many theorists today agree that children are not simply passive recipients of social instruction. Children bring cognition to social experiences and take away something due to both the objective characteristics of situations and their own cognition.

Critics, operating at another level of abstraction, have found standard cognitive theories such as that of Kohlberg (1969) and new socialization theories inadequate proposals. Riegel (1976) has listed several objections, including emphasis on the individual thinker as well as stress on thought as distinguished from action. E. Sullivan (1977) has raised similar questions, pointing out that children have to deal with a social reality based on affective exchanges that may defy rational programming. Simpson (1974) has asked how cognition can have its own developmental course when children in different cultures have to respond to the peculiar societies in which they experience social life.

We see these criticisms as converging on a central issue. When social influences determine thought, the child is reduced to a composite of results from external, determining sources. When cognition is understood to be a structural, self-propelled developmental process, the child remains relatively uninfluenced by society. Thus, these critics are asking: How can a theory account for the truth of both positions? How can the child have his or her thought be socially influenced and, at the same time, construct thought?

## a relational perspective

We have tried to outline a model in which cognition, as self-constructed, and socialization, as determination from without, are each given their due. The outline is broad and as yet empirically unsupported, although there are clear means for assessing its validity (compare Bjornsson, Edelstein, and Kreppner, 1977). These are our essential ideas.

1. Children enter social life seeking order among the events that they experience. They look primarily to interpersonal interactions, episodes in which they exchange actions and reactions with other persons.

2. Children cannot find order in the particular details of interactions, which are, in fact, variable sequences, that are freely composed and not scripted. They can, however, discover order in *general forms* of exchanging behavior, which Piaget (1932) calls *procedures* or *methods* (for example, p. 71) as does Hinde (1976).

3. Procedures of exchange depend on both persons in the interaction. Each can bring his or her respective ideas about exchange to an encounter. If the persons continue to interact together for any amount of time, they will have to reach some agreement about procedures, which will guide them in subsequent interactions.

4. There are several general procedures of interaction that social scientists have identified. Piaget and Sullivan emphasize two. In the first, someone with controlling power imposes a procedure on the child. Piaget calls this *unilateral constraint* and Sullivan calls it *authority*. The child, who attempts to get along with this more powerful person, eventually adopts the appropriate part in this procedure.

5. The most likely person to interact with children in this manner is the adult. Adults are seen as persons who participate in society at large and know from experience about several procedures of exchange, and they bring to children examples of these exchanges. When children construct conceptions of exchanges they experience with adults, they are making self-constructions that simultaneously take account of the concepts held by others persons in society.

6. This process is one way to describe the construction of

thought and the socialization of thought. Procedures of unilateral constraint show the way in which thought is achieved by the individual through collaboration with other persons. It demonstrates why "social cognition" is self-constructed and societally determined.

7. Another procedure important to children's lives is represented by situations in which neither the child nor the other person has unilateral rights of imposition. It applies to cases when two persons are on equal footing, for example, peers and friends. They discover procedures together by making them up through reciprocal exchange. Their collaboration is based on cooperation or coconstruction, in contrast to unilateral imposition.

8. Still, as equals, each person brings to the other a version of social reality. Each, of course, is also participating with several different persons, who are also members of a society. Constructions discovered from interactions with equals who function by reciprocity thus add further to the socialization of thought.

9. Although as developmental psychologists we focus on the child's constructions, we have to recognize that the other in these interactions is also constructing concepts of exchange. It takes two persons to compose exchanges. Even when children seem to be adopting an adult's version of an exchange, they do so from their own understanding, which may differ somewhat from the adult's. In turn, children's conceptions may influence the adult's, and so on throughout their interactive life together.

10. Development, in this model, pertains to discovering exchanges, conceptualizing them as interpersonal relations, and continuing to organize relations with respect to each other and to their application to social reality.

Although it is not the goal of this paper to offer a full model, it can be seen that a cognitive theory need not be at odds with a position on sociological determination. For instance, the foregoing ideas fit a macrosociological theory in which economic relations of exchange determine interpersonal relations and vice versa (Sayer, 1975). This fit is interesting because it admits of socialization without violating the assumption that the cognizing person constructs social reality.

### the Sullivan-Piaget thesis

Sullivan and Piaget are not alone in proposing relation as the analytic unit or in describing it in terms of interactive procedures (compare Hinde, 1976). However, they stand out in drawing developmental implications from the relational starting point. Their thesis is that different types of interpersonal relations which children experience and know serve distinct developmental functions. In particular, relations of unilateral constraint, or authority, serve an educative function that aids children in seeing social reality as lawful and helps them get along with other people. Relations between equals, founded on reciprocal procedures, serves to make children sensitive to other persons and are the main source of mutuality. They become the basis for interpersonal affection and love.

For Sullivan (1953), peer experiences provide the child with "a perfectly novel relationship with the (other) person concerned; he becomes of practically equal importance in all fields of value. Nothing remotely like that has ever appeared before" in development (p. 245). And for Piaget, peer relations provide the child with interpersonal understanding. The personality, or self, that develops from peer relations "takes up its stand on the norms of reciprocity and objective discussion, and knows how to submit to these in order to make itself respected" (pp. 95–96). That is, in peer relations the child "will not only discover the boundaries that separate self from the other person, but will learn to understand the other person and be understood by him" (p. 95).

## studies of friendship

We will now describe some empirical results that bear on relational theory and the Sullivan-Piaget thesis. The studies are part of an ongoing series that we have conducted with subjects ranging in age from six to eighteen years of age. Each study was designed to yield descriptive data that might add substance to the thesis. We also see the data as heuristic, as giving ideas about the important aspects of relations as understood by children. In the sketches of studies to follow, we have adhered to a general rationale in which relations per se have been treated as the topic of social thought. Children have been asked to describe interactions between friends, and we have looked at these descriptions as providing insights into ways that children understand relations.

The broader framework is as follows. The younger the child, the more likely that interpersonal understanding will be in the form of rules about interactions. For example, friends should share; they should not hurt one another. The older the subject, the more clearly relation will be understood as an integrated system of rules. This means that interactions are understood as to their implications for the relation itself. This also means that the relation is known as an ongoing thing whose continued existence depends on the type and sequencing of interactions that the friends participate in and generate.

## defining friendship

Investigators have reported age differences in children's descriptions of friends or peers whom they like (Bigelow and LaGaipa, 1975; Lively and Bromley, 1973; Scarlett, Press, and Crockett, 1971). Children of around six and seven years used terms emphasizing physical characteristics and activities (for example, game playing). Adolescents stressed psychological attributes and general forms of interacting (for example, sharing intimacies). These data have been generally interpreted as manifesting changes in "person perception" or ways of "understanding persons."

We have interviewed approximately 130 children between the ages of six and fourteen years, asking them either: "What is a friend?" or "How does someone show you that they are your friend?" Most children answered these questions by describing examples of interactions that characterize friendship. The developmental trend noted above was supported by our results. The younger the child, the more likely that the interaction described was a physical activity. The older the subject, the more likely the interaction was described in terms of psychological content.

Our data can also be viewed in terms of the Sullivan-Piaget thesis as follows: (1) Children of around six to seven years of age depict friends as interacting according to shared rules of conduct. These rules have the general form: Friends are nice to one another. The rules typically take the specific examples of sharing material goods or playing together. (2) At around age nine to ten years, children use the same rules but predicate them on particular characterizations of the persons in the interactions. For example, sharing is a sign of friendship when one of the friends lacks the thing that the other then supplies. (3) Also at this same age, both friends are described more directly as similar persons. This is done by statements about equality or descriptions of reciprocity in the interaction. (4) Little substantive change is observed in young adolescents of twelve to thirteen years. At best they expand on the persons in the interaction, often adding descriptions of the emo-

tional conditions in which the friends find themselves when the interaction begins.

The following data pertain to a sample of seventy-three subjects
who were asked either to tell how one peer would show another that
they were friends or to tell what a friend is. We will present results by
giving protocols illustrating the above four points.

*Rules.* Twenty-one of twenty-four children, ages six and seven,
described interactions of playing or sharing with minimal reference to
personal characteristics or states of the friends. We call these descriptions *unconditioned* rules. Actual statements include the following:*

(Male, 7 years): *Play with them.*

(Female, 6 years): *Lets me play soccer with him.*

(M, 6): *Somebody that likes you.* (Why is that a friend?) *They
play with him.*

(F, 7): *Someone who likes you.* (?) *Play with them.*

(M, 6): *Because we always go and play with him. Then he
comes and plays with us.*

(F, 7): *Play with them.* (?) *They invite you to a party.*

(M, 6): *A friend is a person you like.* (?) *You play around with
them.*

(F, 7): *Like somebody you know. . . . Play with them; games
like hide-and-go-seek.*

Stories of sharing, which sometimes also involved play, were as
follows:

(M, 6): *They always say yes when I want to borrow their eraser.*

(F, 7): *Play with them; give them stuff.*

(M, 7): *He gave them a lot of stuff and he likes you.* (?) *Play
games.*

(M, 7): *A person that likes another person.* (?) *Give him some of
his candy.* (?) *Play with him.*

*Rules Conditioned on Persons.* Of twenty-six children, ages
nine and ten, ten described interactions in which the act showing
friendship was predicated on a momentary state of need in one of the
peers. Examples include the following:

(F, 9): *If something happened to you, they'd run over to help you.*

(F, 10): *If you're hurt, they come over and visit.*

(M, 9): *You're lonely and your friend on a bike joins you. You
feel a lot better because he joined you.*

---

*Interviewer probe questions not included in text are indicated by (?).

(M, 9): *If you get in trouble, he won't say you did it but stays with you.*

(F, 9): *Somebody that plays with you when you don't have anybody else to play with.*

(F, 9): *When you're lonely, she plays with you.*

(M, 10): *If you need help, like you're hurt, he'll help you or get help.*

(F, 9): *Help someone out. If the other person is stuck, show them the answer but tell them why.*

*Equality and Reciprocity.* Twelve of twenty-six stories contained direct statements of equality or reciprocity within acts showing friendship. Equality was either explicitly described or put in terms of similarities between friends. Here are the four clearest examples:

(M, 9): *It means that he's like a person that is close to you most of the time and helps you do different stuff.*

(M, 10): *Play together all the time. (?) People could be different so they don't have the same feelings as each other and then they don't like each other.*

(M, 10): *The group does things he likes to do. Some kids don't fit in. Last year I played with everybody.*

(M, 10): *Shared everything they had. One wouldn't have more than the other. They'd have everything equal. If one was better than the other one, he wouldn't brag that he was.*

There were eight cases of reciprocity. Here are some clear examples:

(M, 9): *A person who helps you do things. When you need something, they get it. You do the same for them.*

(M, 9): *When I had problems, he helped me and when he had problems, I helped him.*

(F, 10): *She invites me to her house and vice versa.*

(F, 9): *Somebody who can keep your secrets together. Two people who are really good to each other.*

(M, 9): *Somebody that you like and he likes you.*

(M, 10): *Exchange kindness for a long time, not just for a day. Really get to play with each other.*

(F, 9): *They take each other swimming.*

The four children, ages nine and ten, whose descriptions did not fit the above categories gave accounts of rules regarding play comparable to the youngest children.

*Young Adolescents.* There were twenty-three subjects in the twelve- to thirteen-year-old groups. Three described friendship with unconditioned rules of play. Ten subjects predicated acts of friendship on explicit states of deficits in one peer. Four others predicated acts on need and also stressed equality. Five subjects described friends as equals, as similar, or as identical personalities. And one subject emphasized reciprocity.

Examples of stories expressing explicit need were:

(M, 13): *They help you. Like if you're sad, they'll help you feel better.*

(F, 13): *They help you with your problems. They're very loyal to you.*

(M, 13): *When you need help, he helps you. . . . Never turns you down. If another person picks on you, he comes and helps you, if the other is bigger or smaller. Never runs away and leaves you.*

Examples of need plus equality are as follows:

(M, 13): *Someone who knows you and wants to be equal to you. Help you when you're in trouble and wants to come and talk about your problems.*

(F, 12): *They always listen when you have problems. Stick up for you. A friend understands your problems because they go through the same experiences. Even if they can't help, they sympathize.*

Cases of equality are represented by the following protocols:

(F, 12): *They both agree on the same things. You like their personality. Because you have the same ideas, you can talk more freely.*

(F, 13): *Someone you can share things with and who shares things with you. Not material things; feelings. When you feel sad, she feels sad. They understand you.*

The one example of reciprocity was:

(F, 13): *They'll understand your problems. They won't always be the boss. Sometimes they'll let you decide. They'll take turns. If you did something wrong, they'll share the responsibility.*

## interpretation

We see these data as congruent with the Sullivan-Piaget thesis in the following respects. First, children of about six to seven years of age understand the rules by which peers interact as friends in a practical way. These are procedures grounded in functional equality and reciprocity. That is, children of this age level enact these rules when equality means sharing of material goods or doing the same pleasurable activity—playing together. Reciprocity means that sharing and play can be initiated by either peer.

Second, children of age nine to ten years have carried these rules a step further. They have integrated them into a concept of relation. This concept is based on equality and reciprocity, which have become known *principles* of the relation.

Third, this developmental step is accompanied by recognition that the relation is between persons who are individual personalities. Friends are not just peers in general, but particular persons who share ideas, feelings, and interests. Two friends are alike and therefore different in similar ways from other peers who are not their friends.

When the latter two points are combined, we obtain the following picture. Principles of the relation are applied to the individuals in the relation. At this point, interactions become overt signs of friendship; they are behavioral *acknowledgments* of relationship.

For example, several of the middle-age and oldest subjects predicated acts of friendship on deficits in one peer. This can be seen as a statement that the two peers were momentarily unequal. For instance, one was lonely, while the other felt good; one had problems, the other did not; one was hurt, the other well; and so on. Inequality was then an occasion for asserting the principle of equality. The friend who was in a better position performed an act that effectively told the disadvantaged peer that they both merited the better position. This was true even when, as some subjects said, the problem could not be solved. Offering understanding, listening, or sympathizing was a sufficient sign of acknowledgment of the principle of equality.

Lastly, there was little substantive change in concepts of friendship relations between nine to ten years and twelve to thirteen years. The former group seems to have already identified the relation as a topic of knowledge and coupled it with an understanding of the personalities involved. At most we observed that the latter group demonstrates a further articulation of the principles of equality and reciprocity. But they have added little else to the relation except that which comes from further experience and reflective thinking.

### operations for relations

In subsequent interviews conducted with other samples of children, we extended the Sullivan-Piaget thesis along an interesting line. Once friendship is conceived as a relation between personalities of two (or more) peers, interactions take on new significance. They can be understood in an integrated system so that their sequencing functions keep the relation alive. Friendship, or any other social relation, is not a static thing. It is dynamic so that interactions occurring within it cause change. To wit, interactions serve to establish or to disestablish friendship. They seem to maintain friendship or intensify it so that the persons become *best* friends or they serve to deintensify or terminate friendship. They also serve to interrupt the relation momentarily and to repair rifts in order to bring the relation back on course.

We call these *operations* in the broadest sense of the term. In interviewing children about these operations, we have observed the following general result. Six- to seven-year-old children understand each of them, but only in a functional rulelike sense. They do not seem to comprehend the connection between different rules. For example, play is a means for establishing a friendship, while not playing or hitting prevents a friendship from starting or terminates it. Children after about age nine say that a friendship can start when peers get to know one another. Not playing or hitting does not end the relation so easily between friends with like personalities whose bond is based on this similarity.

We will now present a set of data dealing with the integration of two operations: interruption and repair. The data demonstrate the line of development that we think applies to the age range of six to fourteen years. They show the discreteness of young children's rules for interacting and the early adolescent's integration of rules into coordinated systems whose object is the relation itself. Finally, the data indicate the importance of the concept of the individual personalities of the relation, both as a missing element for young children and a pervasive fact for early adolescents.

### violation and repair

We define a violation as an interaction that goes against a rule or principle of a relation. Violations are marked by one or both persons when they note that something has gone wrong or feel that the terms of relation have been broken. If the relation is to be resumed, as it was previously known, one or both persons must work to undo the breach. We call this operation *repair*.

An empirical example is now given based on interviews with thirty-six children, twelve each of ages seven to eight years, ten to eleven years, and twelve to thirteen years. Each subject was first requested to tell a story in which one friend did something that another friend did not like or was bothered by. Next the subject was to describe what the second (offended) person might do, then what the offender might do, and so on until "things were made better and they were friends again."

Nine of the twelve youngest children generated violations in unconditioned, rulelike acts. These included hitting, taking a toy, name calling, and the like. In contrast, eleven of the twelve oldest subjects depicted violations in the context of a stated principle. For instance, one friend did not help another in need; a friend made and then broke a promise; one friend told a third person another friend's secret; and so on. The middle-age group was split between these types of violations.

Of the thirty-six accounts of repair, thirty-one were classifiable according to the schemes described below. There were three general patterns, each of which occurred in two versions (designated below by letters).

*Unprovoked.* In all of these cases, the violation was introduced without mention of a possible impetus. One friend simply did something that the other friend did not like. In version A, offender and offended were assumed to be equals prior to the violation (step 1). The offender then violated a rule; for example, one boy hit another (step 2). The offended friend reacted by becoming angry (step 3). The offender did nothing (step 4). A time lapse followed (step 5). Finally, the friends resumed their normal relation (step 6). When pressed about steps 5 and 6, subjects said: "They don't have to do anything"; "They just forget it"; "No one has to say anything"; "They just laugh it off"; "They just play together"; and so on.

An example of this pattern was the following: One friend took something from another. The latter became angry and told his father. The subject was asked how the boys would become friends again. He said: "When I get mad at my friends, I'm still friends. . . . I don't really know." He was then asked whether one of the peers would have to do anything special. He said: "Sometimes we just keep on playing and see each other and start talking to each other."

The B version of the unprovoked pattern was similar to A through step 3. But at step 4, the offender became angry after the offended friend became angry. At step 5, in answer to the question about who had to do something, subjects said that *both* friends would apologize. They then became friends again.

An example is: "He [Dominic] doesn't like people riding his bike

Ten subjects began stories with specified inequalities between

[but] Freddy goes on riding it." The offended peer reacted by telling Freddy: "You're not gonna ride my bike again." When asked whether they would still be friends, the subject said: "Yeah, if Dominic comes back and he says, 'OK,' and apologizes and. . . ." The interviewer interrupted and asked: "Oh, Dominic apologizes to Freddy?" The subject continued: "Yeah, and then Freddy apologizes and then they keep on playing. . . ."

A total of eighteen children began stories with unprovoked violations. Ten followed pattern A and five followed pattern B. The three other children deviated in saying that the offender alone would have to apologize. Of the fifteen subjects who used A or B, nine were six- to seven-year-olds, and three each came from the middle and oldest groups.

*Unequal.* The second pattern is called *unequal* because stories started with specific statements that the peers were unequal in some relevant respect. For example, one was popular, the other had few friends; one was good at sports, the other was not; one was smart in school, the other was not doing well. In version C, the friends were described as lesser and superior (step 1), and the lesser friend initiated the violation. The offended, superior peer reacted with anger (step 3). There was no immediate counterreaction (step 4), but the offender next initiated repair by offering a verbal apology or compensation (step 5). At step 6, the peers had returned to the initial state of inequality.

An example is: "Sue said she wouldn't tell what Mary had said. She sort of liked this girl so she told her Mary's secrets. . . . Well Mary got mad. . . . Mary has so many friends, one of the most popular girls. Nobody listens to Sue. . . . So Sue is trying to patch things up. [How?] By trying to do things. . . . Sue is going to have a party for her and she tries to be real nice and give her things."

In version D, the friends were described as lesser and superior (step 1) and the superior peer initiated the violation (step 2). The offended, lesser child became angry (step 3). There was no counterreaction (step 4), but on step 5 the *lesser* peer, who was the *offended* party, initiated repair by accepting the violation from the offender. Then the relation returned to its initial inequality.

An example is: "Debbie is really popular. She thinks she's hot stuff. Amy had a crush on the same guy but he liked Debbie, so she went with him. . . . It makes her (Amy) really mad for a while. . . . She would be mad, but she couldn't do anything about it."

Ten subjects began stories with specified inequalities between the friends. Of these, four followed version C and five followed version D. The exceptional case had the superior peer doing the violation and then apologizing. Two, four, and three subjects, respectively, from the three age groups in order of increasing age, used versions C and D.

*Provoked.* In the *provoked* pattern, version E, the violation occurred after an offender had been harmed in some way by the eventual offended peer. Initial equality is assumed, but the first violation breaks it (step 1). Upon being provoked, the offender harmed the other peer (step 2); for example, the offender got the peer into trouble. The offended peer became angry (step 3). No counterreaction occurred (step 4), but in step 5 the offender offered an apology, and the original equality was restored (step 6).

In version F, the offended peer stopped and reflected on the violation after becoming angry (step 4). In thinking about the event, the offended peer reasoned that the offender had not meant to violate their relation. The offended peer then apologized for having gotten angry because a provocation had been falsely assumed.

One of the two cases of false assumption was the following: "[Two boys] did nearly everything together. . . . One day the boy didn't go with Frank fishing. Didn't even tell Frank he was going. [When Frank found out] he said: 'Why didn't you tell me you were going fishing?" . . . He [Frank] told his mother that and she told him that sometimes people like to be by themselves. He [Frank] went to bed that night and thought about that and the next morning he went over to his friend's house and said he was sorry . . . and now he understood what his friend meant when he told him he wanted to be by himself once or twice. And so now they're good friends again."

Eight stories began with a provocation; seven of them followed versions E or F. All of these stories came from the two older groups.

## interpretation

Nine of twelve of the youngest children used the unprovoked pattern, versions A or B, two used the unequal peer pattern, and none the provoked pattern. These results illustrate the general rulelike knowledge children of this age have of peer relations. A violation is of an interactive procedure. Once a violation has occurred, it can be replaced by a rule-abiding interaction. For instance, if hitting is a violation, then playing nicely the next day undoes the violation. If one peer offers an apology, so does the other, even though one peer was an offender and the other was offended. These data illustrate that rules are known but not as part of an integrated system and that rules imply a functional equality and reciprocity (compare version B or the unprovoked pattern).

From about ten years onward, violations required some sort of acknowledgement before the relation could be repaired. The specific work of repair depended on the type of inequality in the friendship or on the provoking circumstances. In cases C through F, the friendship did not simply resume but work had to be done to reinstitute the original relation. This implies knowledge of the relation as such and shows that rules are understood as subordinated to a system wherein one interaction can compensate for another.

The pattern of unequal peers shows the importance of equality as a known principle. When equality is brought to bear on real personalities, the result can sometimes be a factual inequality. Peers differ in popularity, athletic ability, school success, and so on. Friends seem to understand this and apparently agree as to how they can balance the facts with the principle. When the lesser peer initiates the violation, this peer takes on the burden of repair. When the superior peer is the offender, the lesser peer expects no apology and accepts the fact of the other's superiority.

The particular violations in D are worth inspecting because they were not generally direct assaults. Instead, the superior peer took on a boyfriend, promised but did not sit next to someone on a bus trip, competed for and beat out another peer for a position on a team, did not invite a peer to play ball, and made fun of the lesser peer who was a poor hockey player. Only the last, the sole story told by a seven-year-old in this pattern, involved a direct act against a peer. In the other cases, the offender was actually doing something positive, that is, made friends with the boy, sat next to someone on a bus, tried out for a team sport, and started up a game. These acts become violations because of omission rather than commission. They become violations only if the superior peer should have been sensitive to the inequality and was not.

The five version E and two verion F violations are interesting insofar as they pertain to the principle of reciprocity. According to literal reciprocity, if one peer harms another, the other has the right to return the harm. The first then would have the right to initiate further harm, and so the peers could go on hurting one another. When reciprocity is understood as a principle, however, one of the peers is obligated to stop the possible chain. When the peer stops retaliating and offers a positive gesture, the principle of reciprocity requires that the second peer also offer a positive sign. Thus, the peers can return to their normal mode of functioning. In both versions, the negative chain is interrupted by apology, with version F (false assumption) having a tinge of a defense mechanism like rationalization.

## general perspective

These and other data that we have obtained from children have encouraged us to explore the relational thesis further. The results do not simply support the theory, but children in their own words appear to reiterate Sullivan's and Piaget's insightful ideas. We see in the age span sampled here the following points. Procedures with features of equality and reciprocity are understood by young school-age children. Subsequently, these procedures are developed into reorganized systems when the relation proper is characterized by principles. Simultaneously, peers become individualized as personalities and with this we see the modification of principles as they are translated into practical application. Friendship then becomes a relation whose maintenance requires cooperation, a social working together to sustain principles in the face of situational and personal reality.

The agreement of data with theory holds also for specific points of the thesis. Sullivan's definition of interpersonal love can be parsed into the elements of intimacy, similarity in interest, equality of worth, and consensual validation of worthwhileness. Each of these elements is brought out in children's descriptions of friends and how they show one another that they are friends.

Piaget provides the epistemological underpinnings for this developmental course. He proposes that the pragmatic practice of reciprocity between peers "on equal footing" leads to a mutual understanding that interactions based on contraint cannot. Peers do not impose procedures on one another but construct them together. In so doing, they understand what is going on in each other's thoughts and gain mutual respect. We see therefore that after about age nine years, children sense that they think and feel the same as their friends. They are "close," "equal," "fit," or "sympathetic," and share good feelings, emotional problems, and responsibility.

It is not easy to adopt the relational viewpoint or underlying epistemology in the face of contemporary theories of social cognition, which have focused on issues that encourage researchers to analyze development in disparate ways. For the remainder of this essay, we will try to show how these foci differ and how they may be related to one another (compare Youniss, 1977, forthcoming, in press).

*Role Taking.* As we understand current uses of this construct, the key developmental question becomes: When and in which ways are children brought out of egocentrism into knowing what other persons think or feel? This question seems to imply a particular epistemology. Self and other are two individuals, each locked into his or her own inner life. The self-other separation is enhanced by young children's egocentrism. Social knowledge is shared knowledge in the sense that self and other can infer one another's inner life. Thus, the key change in the course of social development occurs when children break out of their own perspectives and learn ways of entering into the perspectives of other persons.

Role taking as an interpersonal process has obvious validity, which any mature adult can verify from his or her own phenomenal experience. This does not, however, support its developmental status. Let us now present the relational alternative.

In Piaget's (1932) epistemology, children from the second year onward recognize that their thoughts and the thoughts of others differ (p. 36). They try to understand these thoughts as they pertain to rules about interaction (p. 52). When the rules are presented to them by means of constraining imposition—which includes cases where adults offer verbal explanations—a peculiar result obtains. Children think they understand the other person, but they do not. Children simply cannot understand the thousands of interactive rules and reasons that adults present and children adopt (p. 89). The result of constraint is an illusion of mutual understanding (p. 36), which is actually a mystification (p. 70). In other words, egocentrism is a *result* of role taking that occurs in relations based on constraint. Piaget (1970) spells this out again and perhaps clarifies the point by reterming this result *sociocentrism* (p. 729).

In contrast to the illusion of mutuality, interactions grounded in reciprocity lead to shared knowledge. Peers actually coconstruct rules and procedures, which become the gist of their relation. Mutuality is first practiced, then reconstituted into principles, and then put back into social practice (Piaget, 1932, p. 98). In other words, peers jointly create the perspectives that they both share. When they take another's perspective, they are taking that which they and the other have constructed. Again, this is reiterated by Piaget (1970), who emphasizes the point that social operations leading to mutual knowledge are in fact *cooperations* (p. 729).

This is not to deny the fact that each of us has a private inner self. It is, however, to bring out clearly that self-and-other comprises a fundamental unit whose reality begins early and whose structure develops. There are at least two types of relational units, and each has its own developmental course, apparently up to adolescence. In the present essay, we have focused on friendship in order to describe the positive functions that it serves in our thesis. What is the long-term product of friendship's development with respect to the individual? For Piaget (1932), the mature self has "admiration for a personality insofar as this personality subjects itself to rules" (p. 98) — not just any rules, but rules based on *reciprocity, sympathy,* and *mutual respect* (p. 196). The ultimate product of a cooperative relation "obliges individuals to 'place' themselves in reciprocal relationship with each other without letting the laws of perspective . . . destroy their individual points of view" (p. 397).

## social thought and social action

By convention, Piaget's theory has been seen as addressing "competence" and being in need of a way to deal with "performance." Kohlberg's theory is frequently used as an example. It is said that Kohlberg describes a subject's moral judgment without being able to predict how the subject will act in a moral situation.

This point of view on cognition may be part of a historical legacy in which development is defined as a general progression from concrete action to increasingly abstract thought. As thought and action become more separated, the question enters as to how the abstract thinker translates thought back into practice (compare Riegel, 1976; E. Sullivan, 1977).

The present model emphasizes the knowledge of relation, where relation is defined as a system of procedures pertaining to interpersonal interactions. Psychological understanding of one's relation to another person is not abstractly separated from one's knowing how to interact with the other person. We see this both in our data on definitions and on violations and repair. Children are able to translate actions into their concept of friendship as is shown in their agreement about which interactions signify friendship. They are able to translate principles of the relation into interaction as is shown in their treatment of equality, inequality, and reciprocity with respect to repair.

We see the children's focus as being on the relation per se. Interactions are understood in terms of their implications for the relation. Children understand interactions as having effects on their relation insofar as particular social behaviors serve to acknowledge, interrupt, or correct it. A concept of relation does not yield a prediction about the precise interaction that the persons will generate. Rather, persons are able to understand the implication of following one instead of another interactive course. They see the results of interaction as bearing on the relation. Effects are anticipated and retrospectively made with the relation as topic and interactions being transformations about it and the various states it can take.

## cognition and affect

It has become a modern aphorism that theories of social cognition have difficulty dealing with affect. This is true if cognition is identified with a kind of objective logic. It need not be the case in the present model. When persons understand the connections between interactions and relations, they know how the results of interactive behavior pertain to the relations between the persons involved.

We refer back to the quoted definitions of friendship offered by children of nine years and older. Several of their descriptions deal explicitly with the results of action on affect. Subjects posit emotional states of loneliness, sadness, or trouble. These feelings are changed by the initiation of interactions. The result is a new emotional state with two explicit components: The peer who was feeling down now feels better, and the two peers share a feeling of understanding.

## summary

Our purpose has been to present a perspective toward social understanding and its development. We have offered neither a complete theory nor decisive data that lead to singular conclusions. We have focused on a brief developmental span and did not look at child-adult relations (compare Damon, 1977).

Historically, social-cognitive theories arose as a criticism of traditional socialization approaches. Presently, social-cognitive theories themselves are being criticized. We see this debate as centering on an important issue: How should the child be characterized? To what degree does the child construct social reality and to what extent does social reality determine the child's constructions?

The perspective that we offer provides a means to address this theme without discarding the positive aspects of both sides. We have tried to show why the child's constructions are self-generated and other-determined. We have also tried to give an epistemological rationale that, we believe, is found in Piaget's writings. And we have attempted to link Piaget's definition of knowledge with Sullivan's account of general social development.

There are several deterrents to accepting this perspective. One opposing view is ideological: Cognition is often assumed to be a self-contained developmental process in which the child, as an individual, accumulates skills for coming to terms with social reality. Another is the assumption that adult-child, especially parent-child, relations are the source of interpersonal sensitivity and affection. A third is the belief that self is at first independent from other and that the development of cognition in the self is the means by which the other comes to be known.

In our view, the Sullivan-Piaget thesis deserves a hearing. It offers a compelling alternative to the common stand on social cognition. The observations that we have collected, some of which we report here, add substance to its key elements. Social thought may be the result of a coconstruction, in the same sense that reactive physical objects cooperate with children who construct space, number, and the like. Self-and-other, like child-and-physical-object, may comprise a basic unit, regarding which children's understanding develops from systems of interactive rules to procedures and eventually into systems of relations.

If accepted, these ideas lead to a novel idea. Child-child and child-adult relations are not simply different, they may be the sources of two types of social understanding with each serving a distinctive developmental function. If children see themselves as living in two types of interpersonal relations, researchers have much work to do in documenting the nature and purpose of these two social worlds of childhood.

## references

Bandura, A. "Social-Learning Theory of Identificatory Process." In D. A. Goslin (Ed.), *Handbook of Socialization Theory and Research.* Chicago: Rand McNally, 1969.

Bigelow, B. J., and LaGaipa, J. J. "Children's Written Descriptions of Friendship: A Multi-Dimensional Analysis." *Developmental Psychology*, 1975, *11*, 857-858.

Bjornsson, S., Edelstein, W., and Kreppner, K. *Explorations in Social Inequality: Stratification Dynamics in Social and Individual Development in Iceland.* Berlin: Max-Planck Institut für Cildungsforschung, 1977.

Damon, W. *The Social World of the Child.* San Francisco: Jossey-Bass, 1977.

Goslin, D. A. *Handbook of Socialization Theory and Research.* Chicago: Rand McNally, 1969.

Hinde, R. A. "On Describing Relationships." *Journal of Child Psychology and Psychiatry*, 1976, *17*, 1-19.

Kohlberg, L. "Stage and Sequence: The Cognitive-Developmental Approach to Socialization." In D. A. Goslin (Ed.), *Handbook of Socialization Theory and Research.* Chicago: Rand McNally, 1969.

Livesly, W. J., and Bromley, D. B. *Person Perception in Childhood and Adolescence.* London: Wiley, 1973.

Piaget, J. "Piaget's Theory." In P. H. Mussen (Ed.), *Carmichaels's Manual of Child Psychology.* Vol. 1. New York: Wiley, 1970.

Piaget, J. *The Moral Judgement of the Child.* New York: Harcourt Press, 1932.

Riegel, K. "The Dialectics of Human Development." *American Psychologist*, 1976, *31*, 689-701.

Sampson, E. F. "Psychology and the American Ideal." *Journal of Personality and Social Psychology*, 1977, *35*, 767-782.

Sayer, D. "Method and Dogma in Historical Materialism." *Sociological Review*, 1975, *23*, 779-819.

Scarlett, H. H., Press, A. N., and Crockett, W. H. "Children's Descriptions of Peers: A Wernerian Developmental Analysis." *Child Development*, 1971, *42*, 439-454.

Shantz, C. U. "The Development of Social Cognition." In E. M. Hetherington (Ed.), *Review of Child Development Research.* Vol. 5. Chicago: University of Chicago Press, 1975.

Simpson, E. L. "Moral Development Research: A Case Study of Scientific Cultural Bias." *Human Development*, 1974, *17*, 81-106.

Sullivan, E. V. "A Study of Kohlberg's Structural Theory of Moral Development: A Critique of Liberal Social Science Ideology." *Human Development*, 1977, *20*, 352-376.

Sullivan, H. S. *The Interpersonal Theory of Psychiatry.* New York: Norton, 1953.

Youniss, J. "The Nature of Social Development." In H. McGurk (Ed.), *Social Development.* London: Methuen, forthcoming.

Youniss, J. "Another Perspective on Social Cognition." In A. Pick (Ed.), *Minnesota Symposium on Child Psychology.* Vol. 9. Minneapolis: University of Minnesota Press, 1975.

*James Youniss is professor of psychology at Boys Town Center, Catholic University, Washington, D.C.*

*Jacqueline Volpe is a graduate student in psychology at Catholic University, Washington, D.C.*

*Children's interpersonal understanding includes two aspects: reflective reasoning and initial orientation. A developmental model sensitive to both aspects is presented.*

# children's use of social conceptions: toward a dynamic model of social cognition

ellen ward cooney
robert l. selman

For the past several years the Harvard-Judge Baker Social Reasoning Project has been studying the child's developing interpersonal understanding.* The research has gone through three phases: descriptive model building, construct validation, and application to other modes of social functioning. As is traditional in structural-developmental research, the goal of the initial phase was to use a stage analysis to describe developmental patterns in children's reflective reasoning. On the basis of extensive clinical interviewing, we outlined a series of five stages of children's conceptions of individuals, friendships, and peer-

---

*Throughout this paper the first person plural is used collectively to refer to contributions made by a number of project members of the past five to seven years. Robert Selman, director of the project, has overseen and participated in all aspects of

group relations. In the second, construct-validation phase, our research was formally designed to evaluate whether these developing stages of reasoning satisfied the essential criteria of structured wholeness, invariant developmental sequence, and universality. Finally, the third phase applied these stage descriptions of reflective reasoning to an analysis of the spontaneous social comments and social interactions of individual children.

The purpose of this paper is to describe these three phases, especially the most recent practical-application phase. An overview of social-cognitive theory, research, and criticism reveals that many individuals working both within and outside the structural-developmental framework have understood this approach to involve only (or mainly) the first two phases of description and validation of stages in reflective reasoning. While we believe that even such a limited approach would be a valid area of investigation, this chapter will suggest that it is now time to go further and use the stage descriptions derived from such descriptive research as a coding scheme for analyzing other modes of social functioning as well. We are suggesting, then, a more dynamic approach to social cognition that analyzes children's reflective reasoning, spontaneous social comments, and social-interaction behaviors with the same developmental-stage descriptions.

## theoretical background:
## the structural-developmental approach

The term *structural development* refers to a set of assumptions and research methodologies common to a number of theories of cognitive and social development. Although the approach finds its roots in

the research. Ellen Cooney has worked on differentiating and outlining the theoretical and methodological implications of reflective reasoning and initial orientation to interpersonal reasoning, and more recently has investigated patterns and processes of stage change. Other project members include: Diane Byrne, who has worked on the structural or perspective-taking component of interpersonal reasoning; Dan Jaquette, who has collaborated on broadening the interpersonal-awareness measurement system, particularly with respect to the peer-group concept, and who is now devising a coding system for analyzing interpersonal reasoning interaction; Debra Lavin, who has begun to look at the natural usage of perspective taking and peer feedback in small groups; Carolyn Newberger, who has begun studying interpersonal awareness in adults with a particular focus on parental awareness of children; Ellie Saunders, who is completing a developmental description of conceptions of the parent-child relationship; and Carolyn Stone, who has begun research on developmental models for examining social-influence strategies. Preparation of this paper was supported in part by a Research Scientist Development Award, K02-MH00157-01, to the second author from the National Institute of Mental Health.

the early interactionist writings of Baldwin (1906) and Mead (1934), the extensive theoretical and empirical work of Jean Piaget (1932, 1952) has provided the basic outline of the theory and much of the present impetus for research in this area. The hallmark of such research is an interest in describing an invariant sequence of cognitively based stages, or qualitatively distinct ways of organizing and understanding a certain domain of experience, through which all children develop. In contrast to other approaches, the focus is on the structure rather than on the content of thought, on universal patterns rather than on individual or situational differences, and on patterns of thinking rather than on emotions or behavior.

Following the pioneering work of Kohlberg (1969) and Flavell (1968), there has been increasing interest in extending this approach to the study of the child's developing understanding of the social world. Most broadly referred to as social cognition, the cognitive-developmental approach to social development has focused on a variety of areas, including moral judgment (Kohlberg, 1976; Rest, 1974); role taking (Flavell, 1968; Kuhn, 1972; Selman and Byrne, 1974); and conceptions of self (Broughton, this volume; Cooney, 1975), social customs, conventions, and institutions (Damon, 1977; Furth, 1976, this volume; Turiel, 1975, this volume). As in structural theory in general, the goals of such social-cognitive studies have been to define qualitatively distinct stages in the child's concepts of various aspects of the social world and to focus on the form of the thinking and on universal patterns related to underlying cognitive structures rather than on affectivity or individual or group differences.

In line with this, the Harvard-Judge Baker Social Reasoning Project was established in 1973 to study the child's developing interpersonal conceptions and to analyze the role taking structure underlying this. Interpersonal conceptions and role taking are not, of course, new areas of study. Social psychologists in the areas of attribution theory, person perception, and role playing have long been interested in these processes in adults (compare Heider, 1958; Kelley, 1973) and occasionally in children (compare Shaw and Sulzer, 1964). As conceptualized in developmental theory, however, role taking and interpersonal conceptions have special meanings that differ considerably from many previous uses (Selman, 1976a). From this perspective, role taking (here referred to as *social-perspective taking* to distinguish it from these other uses) refers to the process by which a person is able to take the perspective of another and relate it to his or her own perspective. Developmentally, social-perspective taking is viewed as beginning at a level at which the child fails to distinguish social viewpoints of self and other. It then develops in a series of regular steps, first distinguishing these perspectives and then relating them to each other in progressively more complex ways. As this provides the basic structure underlying the child's developing interpersonal understanding, our interest in interpersonal conceptions is closely tied to this. As described by an early member of the Social Reasoning Project, the structural study of interpersonal conceptions and perspective taking entails "the derivation of a sequence of logically-related structures or forms which individuals display in their understanding of others. The concern is not with content, not with accuracy or behavioral choice, but with the form in which perspectives of others emerge, or the reasons for behavioral choice. The focus is not on what emotion or trait an individual attributes to another on the basis of some information about him, but on what the process is by which an individual becomes able to make such inferences about another" (Byrne, 1973, p. 349).

As a group of developmental psychologists, child therapists, and educators, our goal was both to increase our general knowledge about the development of social understanding and to investigate how this could be put to use in clinical and educational assessment and intervention.

## phase 1:
## basic developmental descriptive research

The initial purpose of the Social Reasoning Project was to describe a series of stages in children's developing interpersonal conceptions. As structural developmentalists, our interest was in universal and invariant developmental changes in general patterns of children's understanding and thinking. The goal of the first phase of research, then, was to develop a formal model that would reflect both our empirical data about a variety of children's developing social conceptions and a logical analysis of the perspective-taking structure underlying them.

The first task in developing this model was to define the specific concepts to be studied. Quite clearly, there is no one way to divide the domain of interpersonal conceptions. As Selman has recently written, "There may be as many ways to map social cognition as there are map makers" (Selman, Jaquette, and Lavin, 1977, p. 266). The decision, then, must be based on one's particular area of concern. Our own special focus reflects our clinical interest in children's developing understanding of the nature of individuals and in their growing ability to develop and maintain effective peer relations.

The specific concepts of study were chosen with both practical and theoretical considerations. From a theoretical perspective, we wanted to concentrate on issues generally recognized as important in the study of interpersonal relations. As Flavell (1974, p. 67) has noted:

> There tends to be something less than adequate inter-change and mutual stimulation between the social psychologists who study the various forms of adult social cognition and the developmental psychologists who investigate the growth of the same or similar forms during childhood and adolescence. While developmental work is sometimes cited by the specialist in adult social cognition . . . one suspects that, with occasional exceptions, it plays little role in his thinking about the topic. More importantly, perhaps, research on social-cognitive growth is only rarely explicitly shaped and guided by research and theory in the corresponding adult field.

As one step in attacking this problem, a careful survey was made of the social-psychological literature to delineate areas of greatest interest (Bruss-Sanders, 1977; Selman and Jaquette, forthcoming). From a practical point of view, we then selected from these sources the issues that seemed most relevant to the special interpersonal concerns of children—particularly children experiencing interpersonal difficulties.

As a result, to date we have focused our study of interpersonal understanding on three main areas: conceptions of individuals, conceptions of close dyadic friendships, and conceptions of peer-group relations. Furthermore, within each of these areas a more refined set of issues was defined. Included in the area of individuals are the issues of subjectivity, self-awareness, personality, and personality change. Under friendship are formation, closeness, trust, jealousy, conflict, and termination. Finally, the issues within peer-group relations include formation, cohesion-loyalty, conformity, rules and norms, decision making, leadership, and termination. (See Table 1 for a summary of these issues.)

As is typical in social-cognitive research, we have used a semi-structured clinical interview to investigate patterns in children's developing ideas about these issues. To study developmental changes in

## Table 1. Issues of Interpersonal Awareness Related to
## Conceptions of the Individual, Close Friendships,
## and Peer-Group Organization

| Individual | Friendship | Peer Group |
|---|---|---|
| 1. *Subjectivity:* covert properties of persons (thoughts, feelings, motives); conflicts between thoughts or feelings within the person | 1. *Formation:* why (motives) and how (mechanisms) friendships are made; the idea of friend | 1. *Formation:* why (motives) and how (mechanisms) groups are formed; the ideal member |
| 2. *Self-Awareness:* awareness of the self's ability to observe its own thoughts and actions | 2. *Closeness:* types of friendship, ideal friendship, intimacy | 2. *Cohesion-Loyalty:* group unity |
| 3. *Personality:* stable or predictive character traits | 3. *Trust:* doing things for friends; reciprocity | 3. *Conformity:* range and rationale |
| 4. *Personality Change:* how and why people change (growing up) | 4. *Jealousy:* feelings about intrusions into new or established relationships | 4. *Rules and Norms:* types of rules and reasons for them |
| | 5. *Conflicts:* how friends resolve problems | 5. *Decision Making:* setting goals, resolving problems, working together |
| | 6. *Termination:* how friendships break up | 6. *Leadership:* its qualities and its function in the group |
| | | 7. *Termination:* why groups break up or members are excluded |

friendship concepts, for instance, we present in either filmstrip or verbal form a dilemma in which a child has been asked by a newcomer in town to go to a special event that, unfortunately, conflicts with a previously settled plan with a long-time chum. In this dilemma, the first child, Kathy, has been asked by a new girl to go to an ice skating show with her the next afternoon, and this conflicts with a date with Kathy's best friend, Debby, to plan a puppet show. To complicate matters, Debby does not like the new girl. Likewise, in studying peer-group conceptions, we present situations in which the child must decide which of two groups to join or choose between self and group interests. Following the presentation of each dilemma, we ask the child a flexible series of questions related to the specific issues in the story. In the friendship dilemma above, for instance, the child discusses how friendships are formed in the story, whether Kathy's decision to go to the ice show might break her friendship with Debby, whether Debby might be jealous and how this might affect their friendship, and so on. Each of these questions, moreover, is used as a starting point from which to investigate the child's reasoning about related issues in personal experience. By having children of differing ages apply to specific situations their understanding of such issues as how friendships are formed or maintained, we are able to study underlying regularities of thought and to outline developmental changes in them.

From interviewing subjects from preschool through adolescence and into adulthood in this manner, we have outlined five stages of development in each of these seventeen issues of interpersonal awareness. The result is a stage-by-issue model of developing interpersonal conceptions. This model both describes the separate development of each of the seventeen issues and suggests logical or structural parallels across the various issues, allowing comparison of the child's stage of reasoning on one issue with his or her stage on another. (See Table 2 for an outline of the basic characteristics of conceptions of individuals, friendships, and peer groups at each stage. A more detailed description is found in Selman and Jaquette, 1977.)

Let us illustrate with a comparison of the parallel development of two issues: trust in friendships and loyalty in peer-group relations.

**Table 2. General Characteristics of Stages Across Conceptions of Individuals, Friendships, and Peer Groups**

| Stage | Individual | Friendship | Peer Group |
|-------|-----------|-----------|-----------|
| 0 | Physical entity | Momentary physical playmate | Physical connections |
| 1 | Intentional subject | One-way assistance | Unilateral relations |
| 2 | Introspective self | Fair-weather cooperation | Bilateral partnerships |
| 3 | Stable personality | Intimate-mutual sharing | Homogeneous community |
| 4 | Complex self-systems | Autonomous interdependence | Pluralistic organization |

At stage 0, children equate trust with physical capabilities. For example, four-year-old Alan said that he trusted his best friend because, "if I give him my toy he won't break it . . . he isn't strong enough." A similar physical focus is found in stage 0 conceptions of group loyalty. Asked how one keeps someone in a group, one five-year-old said, "You have to all hold hands to keep them together." At stage 1 in both trust and loyalty, children realize that it is feelings and intentions and not just physical characteristics that keep relationships and groups together. But this still remains a one-way street. As one stage 1 child said, "You trust a friend if he does what I want." Likewise, a stage 1 understanding is seen in an eight-year-old's description of loyalty as "always doing what your friend wants, 'cause they can kick you out if you don't." At stage 2 in both conceptions, this notion is expanded to include a consideration of both parties. For instance, one nine-year-old said, "Trust means if you do something for him, he'll do something for you." Similarly, loyalty to a group is viewed in terms of equalizing "deals" and mutual relationships that benefit both the individual and the group. Similar comparisons can be made for all five stages across each of the seventeen issues of interpersonal conceptions.

## phase 2: validating the model

The result of the first constructive phase of research, then, is a formal stage-by-issue model of reasoning derived from both empirical research and structural analysis. The goal of the second phase is to evaluate whether children's developing interpersonal conceptions actually fit this stage model. To do this, data are gathered more formally and evaluated to determine whether or how well children's interpersonal reasoning meets the stage criteria of structured wholeness, invariant sequence, and universality.

First, let us consider the structured wholeness of interpersonal conceptions. To begin investigating this, we have studied the consistency of the individual's stage of reasoning both on similar issues in different dilemmas and across the different issues within any one dilemma. The evidence gathered so far is generally supportive. For example, in a study comparing the reasoning of forty-seven preadolescent boys on four different dilemmas, the correlations between conceptions of individuals and relationships ranged from 0.71 to 0.99 across dilemmas (Selman, 1976b). In subsequent testing two years later and in a reanalysis of the original data with a slightly revised scoring system, factor analyses showed that a single factor accounted for over 60 percent of the variation in stage scores across the seventeen issues at each time and that no other factor accounted for over 14 percent of the variance (Selman and Jaquette, forthcoming).

We have also begun to investigate the claim of invariant developmental sequence. In general, longitudinal and cross-sectional analyses of interpersonal reasoning data gathered through interview procedures show a progressive age-related development through childhood and adolescence and provide no evidence of regression or of misordering in the developmental model (Selman and Jaquette, forthcoming; Selman, Jaquette, and Lavin, 1977). Table 3, for instance, presents the overall age range of 231 subjects found at each stage of reasoning and shows a clear age-related pattern. Table 4 shows the stage scores of forty-eight six- to twelve-year-old subjects in 1974 and again in 1976. As can be seen, eight of the forty-eight subjects remained at the same stage over this two-year period, while the other forty subjects made gains varying from one-third of a stage to a full stage. No subject evidenced regression in reflective-reasoning stages. One follow-up study, of course, does not provide sufficient data to test the assumption of invariant sequence adequately. Nonetheless, the data gathered so far are supportive.

Finally, while cross-cultural data best provide the type of evidence necessary for judging how adequately the developmental model captures the universal features of interpersonal reasoning, research of this nature requires considerable anthropological as well as developmental dedication; our work has not yet been extended in this direction. Another approach to validating the claim of universality is to look at samples where one might expect to find differing patterns. Our

Table 3. Age Range of Subjects at Each Stage
of Interpersonal Reasoning (N = 231)

| Stage | Age Range (years:months) | Number of Subjects |
|---|---|---|
| 0 | 2:4–5:11 | 6 |
| 1 | 4:6–12:4 | 60 |
| 2 | 6:9–15:10 | 98 |
| 3 | 11:3–adulthood | 31 |
| 4 | 17:8–adulthood | 36 |

### Table 4. Overall Interpersonal Reasoning Stage at Initial Interview and at Two-Year Follow-Up

| Initial Interview Stage | Follow-Up Interview Stage[a] | | | | | | |
|---|---|---|---|---|---|---|---|
| | 1 | 1 (2) | 2 (1) | 2 | 2 (3) | 3 (2) | 3 |
| 1 | 1 | 3 | 4 | 2 | – | – | – |
| 1 (2) | – | 2 | 4 | 3 | – | – | – |
| 2 (1) | – | – | – | 8 | 1 | – | – |
| 2 | – | – | – | 5 | 4 | 8 | 1 |
| 2 (3) | – | – | – | – | – | 1 | 1 |
| 3 | – | – | – | – | – | – | – |

[a]Numbers in parentheses indicate subjects' secondary stage of reasoning in cases where evidence exists for more than one reasoning stage.

research pertinent to this is a longitudinal comparative study of twenty-one "emotionally-disturbed" children in a special clinic school matched case by case with public school peers on the basis of sex, race, social class, and psychometric intelligence (Selman, 1976b). While the average stage of reflective reasoning was significantly lower among the clinic group at two separate testing periods (as a group the lag was from two to three years), the responses of the clinic sample fit within the system. A two-year longitudinal follow-up of their development yielded the same general findings as with the forty-eight subjects in the normative study: a general movement upward with no sign of regression in interpersonal-reasoning stages.

Clearly, such data are only an initial step in establishing the applicability of stage analysis to developing interpersonal conceptions. Moreover, as the descriptive research continues, the model will need continual reevaluation. Nonetheless, the evidence to date provides sufficient support to encourage our further efforts at extending and applying this developing stage model of reflective reasoning to other modes of functioning as well. It is to a discussion of these that we now turn.

## phase 3: application to other modes of functioning

The first two phases of our research have involved the development and continuing evaluation of a model of interpersonal conceptions. This model provides a stage-by-issue outline of general patterns in children's developing thinking about individuals, friendships, and peer groups. We believe this to be valuable in itself. Just as Piaget's investigations were motivated by the desire to understand the development of knowledge about the physical and logical-mathematical world, we believe that social-cognitive research can provide valuable insight into children's developing understanding of the social world (compare Damon, 1977). Further, by comparing the patterns and processes in the understanding of the social and the nonsocial worlds, we may learn more about general patterns of cognitive development as well as about patterns unique to thinking in each domain.

Nevertheless, we believe that this model remains limited in that it deals only with general patterns in the child's *reflective reasoning*. The purpose of this section is to suggest the potential value of going beyond development of this model to a third phase of research that analyzes how children actually use or apply these same patterns of understanding in other aspects of their social functioning as well. More specifically, we will suggest that it is possible to distinguish three related modes of social functioning to which this model of social understanding may be applied: (1) reflective reasoning—the thoughtful, probed responses to an interpersonal problem or dilemma; (2) initial interpersonal orientation—the child's first or spontaneous responses to such interpersonal questions (responses that reflect the child's general awareness and sensitivity to the social issues under investigation); and (3) reasoning in action—the child's naturally occurring social comments and social-interaction patterns.

*Reflective Reasoning.* We begin by looking at reflective reasoning itself. As noted, this refers to the carefully probed reflective responses that a child verbalizes about his or her interpersonal understanding in response to an interviewer's questions about hypothetical or real interpersonal situations. It is this kind of reasoning that was used in our initial model development (phases 1 and 2) and that is commonly studied by other social-cognitive researchers (compare Broughton, this volume; Kohlberg, 1969; Turiel, 1975, this volume).

The nature of this understanding will be clarified by looking more closely at the methods used to evaluate it. Although a variety of procedures have been used, most involve presenting the child with an interpersonal problem or dilemma and probing his or her reasoning about it. In our basic research, for instance, the child's stage of reasoning about persons has frequently been evaluated with the following dilemma:

Eight-year-old Tom is trying to decide what to buy his friend Mike for his surprise birthday party. By chance, he meets Mike on the street and learns that Mike is extremely upset because his dog, Pepper, has been lost for two weeks. In fact, Mike is so upset that he tells Tom, "I miss Pepper so much I never want to look at another dog again." Tom goes off, only to pass a store with a sale on puppies; only two are left and these will soon be gone. The dilemma, then, is whether to buy the puppy for Mike, and how this will affect their friendship.

As is typical in structural-developmental research, the interview using this dilemma covers a range of related issues basic to the child's developing conceptions of persons. Each issue has a basic orienting question followed by a series of relatively standard probe questions designed to elicit further explanation and clarification of the child's reasoning. For example, to explore the issue of self-awareness, we start with a general question such as "Mike said he never wants to see another puppy again. Why did he say that?" Depending in part on the child's initial level of response, the experienced interviewer might choose from a range of stage-related follow-up questions such as: "Can someone say something and not mean it?"; "Is it possible that Mike doesn't know how he feels?"; "Can you ever fool yourself into thinking you feel one way when you really feel another?"; and so on. In addition to providing the stimuli for the child's discussion of his or her general understanding of the issue, these questions also test the child's ability to take different aspects of the situation into consideration, to make discriminations and integrations not originally made, and so forth.

As is common practice, the subject's complete set of responses to each interview is transcribed and given a stage score. Unfortunately, we clearly cannot claim that this adequately taps the child's interpersonal reasoning ability. No such unidimensional verbal technique could. Nonetheless, the procedures does give the child both permission and encouragement to reflect on the issue carefully and to come up with thoughtful reasoning about it. It is this that is measured by the reflective-reasoning stage score.

*Initial Orientation to Interpersonal Reasoning.* There is, however, a second dimension or mode of interpersonal reasoning that can be analyzed with these interview methods. This is the child's *initial* response to the first, or orienting, question about each issue. It should be recalled that following the initial question, the interviewer probes the child's understanding, pushing the subject to make various distinctions, to reason in more complex ways, and so on. By doing this kind of probling, we have argued, we are evaluating—within, of course, the constraints of the child's verbal ability—the child's best interpersonal understanding. However, there may often be a discrepancy between the stage at which the child can reason on a reflective interview and his or her initial performance—that is, between the aspects of a situation he or she *spontaneously* focuses on and how he or she *initially* reasons about this issue. Rather than revealing the highest interpersonal reasoning that the child is able to produce when pushed to reflect carefully on his or her ideas, this initial orientation is closer to social-psychological notions of attitude than to structuralist notions of stage. The distinction, in fact, appears closely related to Flavell's (1968, 1977) differentiation between existence and need: A child may have an underlying reasoning ability (existence) but simply not be inclined to use this (need) in a specific situation. Yet this initial orientation can be evaluated with the same stage analysis used to measure reflective reasoning. Doing so, we believe, can allow useful comparisons of reasoning in these two modes of interpersonal functioning.

An example from a recent intervention study involving ninety-six second and third grade children (Cooney, 1978) may clarify this. A major difference between stage 1 and stage 2 conceptions of subjectivity—one of the issues in the "individual" category—is that the stage 2 child realizes that an individual may have two feelings at the same time, while the stage 1 child does not.* This is because the stage 1 child still concretizes emotions: Feeling happy and sad at the same time is akin to being in New York and Chicago at the same time. In this study, one way of evaluating the child's conception of subjectivity in response to the dilemma described above is by probing his or her understanding of the birthday boy's feelings if he gets the puppy as a present. The stage 2 child will understand that he may be both happy and sad: happy about the new dog, but sad about his old one who is lost. The stage 1 child, however, believes that Mike could only feel one way: either happy or sad, but not both. However, it was not uncommon for children capable of stage 2 conceptions to respond to this issue initially

---

*It should be noted that references to "stage 1 child" or "stage 2 child" are really shorthand ways of referring to "a child who gives a stage 1 (or stage 2) response about this issue." As should be progressively clearer as we discuss the various modes of functioning to which stage analyses can be applied, it is the reasoning, not the child, that can be appropriately staged.

by focusing only on one emotion and not spontaneously recognizing the need to consider that Mike could feel two ways. Only later during the interview did such children reveal their stage 2 awareness that Mike could in fact feel both happy and sad at the same time.

In making this distinction between reflective reasoning and initial orientation in evaluating the interview protocols in this intervention study, a number of interesting differences appeared (Cooney, 1978). For reflective reasoning, the individual child's scores were highly correlated across the different issues and over time (averaging 0.62 and 0.63, respectively). The initial-orientation scores lacked this close relationship and stability (0.10 and 0.34, respectively), suggesting that there is more individual and situational fluctuation in children's tendency to use their best level of understanding than there is in their understanding itself. In addition, for the group as a whole, the initial-orientation stage was below that of reflective reasoning. An informal survey of the patterns for each child showed that this was a common pattern for the individual as well as the group, but this was by no means a consistent pattern for all subjects. In other words, in considering a problem more carefully, some children generally came up with a higher stage reasoning than that initially used, while others did not show this disparity.

In conclusion, although logically we might expect that a child should be able to use the same stage in both reflective reasoning and initial orientation, this is not always the case. Of course, a child who eventually reveals a higher stage of reasoning than that initially used cannot be said to lack this higher-stage understanding. But it can be said that he or she tends not to use this when not pushed to do so. This would seem to have a number of implications for both diagnosis and remediation of children experiencing interpersonal difficulties. Some of these will be considered in the final section of this paper. Clearly, though, a great deal more research is needed to chart the relationship between these two modes of functioning and to understand the causes and consequences.

## social reasoning in action

Despite the differences between the two modes of functioning, both reflective-reasoning scores and initial-orientation scores measure the child's verbal reasoning in response to an artificial test situation. One of the major criticisms of structural theory is its almost exclusive focus on reasoning to the neglect of social behavior. What, critics ask, can this approach tell us about social behavior, which is really the interest of social developmentalists? Although we believe that social reasoning is a valid area of investigation in itself, we also recognize the importance of studying social behavior. This becomes particularly important, in fact, when one's interest turns from basic descriptive research about social reasoning to an application of developmental descriptions to the diagnosis and remediation of individuals with interpersonal problems.

In line with this, project members have been exploring whether our model of reflective reasoning can be used to analyze social reasoning in action, including both the child's spontaneous comments in naturally occurring social situations and his or her social behavior. More specifically, we have begun trying to use the social-cognitive map of social-conceptual stages as a social-cognitive developmental coding scheme for the analysis of both naturally-occurring peer-group discussions and children's social-interaction strategies.

Although we hope to study both normal and clinic populations, our present research site is a clinic school within the Judge Baker Guidance Center in Boston. This school is both an educational and a psychological treatment center for learning and emotionally disabled children between the ages of seven and fifteen. A major difficulty for these children is disturbance in interpersonal relationships, particularly in peer relations. As a result, included in the program are a variety of situations that encourage the children to provide support and feedback to each other within the context of their peer group. Programs are designed to help children help each other with problems surrounding such issues as cooperation, conflict resolution, and making friendships. As can be seen, many of these issues are included in our stage-by-issue map of developing interpersonal reasoning.

Within this general context, we have been studying the child's reasoning in action in four main settings: a weekly interpersonal problem-solving session in which children evaluate their week's performance along such issues as cooperation, conflict resolution, and decision making; small weekly groups for planning trips or other activities; regular current-events classes; and intermittent discussions with school counselors about classroom difficulties.

Several kinds of data are gathered. First, the discussions just described are tape recorded, transcribed, and scored. Second, on occasion during the formative research phase, the same children are individually interviewed with the reflective-reasoning interview described previously. Finally, records of the actual social interactions and behavior of these children across various situations are kept.

Eventually, we expect these data to provide types of information related to the stability and deviation of interpersonal-reasoning stage across different modes of functioning. These include: (1) a comparison of the individual's reasoning stage on reflective interviews and on reasoning in action about the same issues, (2) a comparison of the average reasoning stage in small-group discussions with children of differing average ages or levels of social competence, and (3) a comparison of the reasoning stage of individuals and groups over temporally proximate situations (for example, within a period of several weeks).

Our general impression from this research is that it is possible to reliably interpret many aspects of children's comments and behavior in terms of the issues and stages in our reflective model. To illustrate the kinds of information we are gathering, we shall describe the cases of two twelve-year-old boys, whom we shall call John and Jerry. On his reflective interview, John's reasoning was stage 2 almost consistently across all seventeen issues. On the specific issue of leadership, for example, he said that a good leader was "someone who helps the members cooperate with one another, and who resolves conflict when group members disagree." However, when John actually had an opportunity to be a class leader, he became very anxious and refused, telling a counselor, "I'm not going to be the class leader because nobody will do what I tell them to do." When the counselor then asked what a good leader would be like, John replied, "Someone who everyone else did what he wanted." This reasoning can easily be scored at stage 1, in which a leader is described as an arbitrary controller. John's stage 1 reasoning in action, then, contrasted markedly with his stage 2 reflective reasoning, which was produced in the apparently less anxiety-ridden interview.

A different relationship between these two modes of functioning was demonstrated by Jerry. This child showed a relatively consistent pattern of one-way, stage 1 reasoning on the reflective interviews. Leaders for him were people who could "boss others around." However, when it was Jerry's turn to be class leader, he appeared to show a more mature stage 2 understanding. Rather than trying to force his will on others, Jerry appeared to be trying to mediate the group decision making process, taking a more reciprocal, stage 2 perspective in the role of a leader.

The case of a sixteen-year-old named Tommy illustrates another aspect of this system: changes in social-interaction strategies that can be understood in terms of stage development. When first admitted to the clinic school, Tommy, who had a history of severe social deprivation and abuse, frequently hid under his desk for fear of teachers and peers. Gradually, however, he began to form a close tie to his teacher; but this tie was based almost entirely on a one-sided "you give, I take" basis, characteristic of a stage 1 child's understanding of the nature of friendships. After a year, Tommy then formed his first real peer relation. Rather than being based on what is usually a common bond of trust (stage 3)—Tommy's relationship was based on playing and sharing toy trucks with another, younger child in the class. This relationship also exemplified a stage 1, one way notion of friendship as the give and take of activities and possessions. In his occasional attempts to make new friends, Tommy would approach a child with a toy to share, or would go up to other children and try arbitrarily to join in their play. If the others did not respond in kind, Tommy would become upset and leave, not realizing the effect of his own inadequate social strategies. Further, the occasional child who attempted to engage Tommy in a more age-appropriate way of forming and maintaining friendships, for example, by a mutual sharing of ideas, feelings, or activities, was not responded to and would give up the effort.

We have presented these anecdotes to illustrate that it is possible both to code some aspects of social-interaction strategies in structural terms and to demonstrate some of the interesting patterns of similarities and differences that emerge across modes of functioning when this comparative analysis is done. Tommy's behavior, for example, clearly illustrates the stage 1, one-way notion of friendship formation. When other children who appeared to demonstrate a higher-level understanding of making friends approached him, Tommy was not able to respond in kind. Hence no relationship was formed. Our stage-by-issue map appears to be able to help us not only to understand developmental patterns in reflective reasoning but also to place Tommy's behavior along a developmental continuum. Rather than leading us to focus on his rebuff of the other children, it leads us to look at Tommy's social-interaction strategies and to see him not simply as hostile or "unfriendly," but as a child whose way of making friends is developmentally behind the way of his peers. The cases of John and Jerry also illustrate how one can interpret behavior in terms of stages of leadership concepts; and these cases illustrate the usefulness of this model in highlighting stage differences between reflective reasoning and reasoning in action. With John, the anxiety of the leadership role seemed to cause him to lose sight of his more mature understanding. Jerry, conversely, moved beyond his usually lower-stage verbal reasoning when actually in a leadership role. Although such data provide information only about the pattern and not about the cause, they raise interesting questions about the influences and constraints of the leadership and the interviewee roles that may lead to such a discrepancy. In the concluding section of this paper, we turn to a consideration of these and other implications of these efforts to analyze several modes of social reasoning with the same social-cognitive model.

## conclusions and implications for future research

This chapter has described our basic research on the development of interpersonal conceptions and outlined some new directions that we are pursuing. The study has gone through three phases: developmental descriptive model building, construct validation, and application of the model to the analysis of other modes of functioning. While work continues on each phase, particular emphasis has been placed on practical application, and we have described our efforts to analyze reflective reasoning, initial orientation, and reasoning in action. Throughout, our goal has been to show that our developmental model of social cognition can be used to analyze other modes of social functioning as well.

This effort to differentiate several related modes of functioning and to analyze all with the same stage model has a number of implications for theory, research, and intervention. While some implications have been alluded to in previous sections, we will conclude by outlining several of the more important ones. Although the discussion is centered on our own work in interpersonal conceptions, we believe that these general considerations are equally applicable to other areas of social-cognitive research as well.

First, we have suggested that interpersonal reasoning, even on a purely verbal interview level, is not a unitary construct that one measures or does not measure. We have, in fact, distinguished two ways of analyzing such reasoning—reflective reasoning and initial orientation—and have argued that each reveals something different about the child's social understanding. This suggests the need for particular awareness of the mode of reasoning actually being evaluated with verbal measures and also the need for considerable caution in interpreting group or individual differences. Less verbal children, for instance, could unfairly receive lower scores than their more verbal counterparts, not because of a difference in reflective reasoning but because of the different depth of reasoning reached in the assessment. The same holds true for children who become bored by the interview, are uncomfortable with the interviewer, or who have difficulty reflecting on their reasoning and speak more impulsively. Different amounts of probing by different interviewers could produce similar problems and would further emphasize the need for interviewers blind to treatment conditions, as well as the need for a standardized amount of probing.

A second set of implications involves the relationship between social reasoning and social behavior. Although there has been considerable interest in this, the relationship has generally been found to be inconsistent and difficult to conceptualize and has therefore led many to question the value of the structuralist focus on reasoning. The analysis presented here suggests that instead of comparing broad categories of reasoning and behavior (for example, interpersonal reasoning with helping behavior or moral reasoning with moral behavior), it would be more appropriate to analyze the understanding of specific issues such as leadership roles or friendship formation and to compare these with directly related social behavior such as the actual attempt to make friends or lead a group. We have presented several examples of this kind of comparison. Clearly the same could be done for each of the issues in our model or, indeed, for any other issue where the child's developing understanding was amenable to a similar stage analysis.

Further, by providing a common vocabulary for analyzing aspects of reflective reasoning, initial orientation, and behavior, this model allows us to examine both similarities and differences in stage usage across these modes. By looking at similarities, we can begin to study more directly the nature of the relationship between interpersonal reasoning, awareness, and behavior—areas that have typically been evaluated with very different measures. Our guess is that such research would show that when both are analyzed within a stage model, the child's reflective reasoning would most often be at the same or at a higher stage than his or her behavior and that the interpersonal orientation stage would fall somewhere in between. This expectation arises from the assumption that there may be other external factors influencing orientation and behavior besides reflective reasoning and that these might vary more widely across individuals and situations.

Looking at the differences in stage across these modes of functioning, conversely, would provide a useful way to begin investigating what some of the factors might be that influence the child's social functioning in each of these three areas. In other words, by using our stage descriptions as a standard against which to measure children's reflective reasoning, initial orientation, and reasoning in action, we can start comparing the stage of understanding revealed by different individuals across different situations in each of these three modes. This should allow us to begin generating hypotheses about the factors that influence — either positively or negatively — children's social reasoning in each mode of functioning. We might find, for instance, that impulsive children show a large disparity between their reflective reasoning and their initial orientation and behavior, while more reflective children do not. Likewise, it is possible that situational conditions of responsibility might serve to raise the stage of some children's social behavior when they believe that their actions might really make a difference. But these same conditions might lower the functioning of others who become too anxious to function at their best.

Finally, similar comparisons of reasoning across these three modes of functioning might aid in our understanding of and intervention with individual children having interpersonal behavior problems. Perhaps, in fact, intervention strategies themselves should vary according to the relationship between the child's reflective reasoning, initial orientation, and reasoning in action. When all these are at the same stage, an approach focusing on cognitive-stage change might be most appropriate. The child is already using his or her reasoning ability in these other areas, and the goal would be to stimulate change to a higher social-cognitive stage. Conversely, in situations where initial orientation lags behind reflective reasoning, cognitive-stage change does not appear as important. Intervention might better focus on increasing the child's spontaneous tendency to use his or her social understanding, applying such methods as direct teaching, social awareness, or sensitivity training. Finally, where the stage of social interaction lags behind the other two, other techniques, including modeling and the reinforcement of different behavior patterns might be the most effective kind of social intervention.

In closing, we should emphasize that not all aspects of interpersonal reasoning, orientation, or behavior are amenable to the kind of stage analysis and comparison described here. The child's interpersonal knowledge, attitudes, and behavior are wonderfully complex and cannot be reduced to five stages of reasoning. We believe, however, that this dynamic stage analysis of interpersonal functioning is one useful way of beginning to unravel some of these complexities. Our investigations have only just begun. They have left us with more questions than answers, more speculation than fact. Our hope is simply that others may find these possibilities as intriguing as we do.

## references

Baldwin, J. M. *Thought and Things.* 3 vols. London: Swann Sonnenschein, 1906-1911.

Bruss-Sanders, E. "The Development of Children's Understanding of Parent-Child Relationships." Unpublished manuscript, Harvard-Judge Baker Social Reasoning Project, Harvard University, 1977.

Byrne, D. "The Development of Role-Taking in Adolescence." Unpublished doctoral dissertation, Harvard University, 1973.

Cooney, E. W. "Social Cognitive Development: An Experimental Intervention in the Elementary Grades." Unpublished doctoral dissertation, Harvard University, 1978.

Cooney, E. W. "The Child's Conception of Self Identity: Implications from Cognitive Developmental Theory." Unpublished manuscript, Harvard University, 1975.

Damon, W. *The Social World of the Child.* San Francisco: Jossey-Bass, 1977.

Flavell, J. H. *Cognitive Development.* Englewood Cliffs, N.J.: Prentice-Hall, 1977.

Flavell, J. H. "The Development of Inferences about Others." In T. Mischel (Ed.), *Understanding Other Persons.* Oxford: Blackwell, Basil, Mott, 1974.

Flavell, J. H. *The Development of Role-Taking and Communication Skills in Children.* New York: Wiley, 1968.

Furth, H. "Children's Conception of Social Institutions: A Piagetian Framework." *Human Development,* 1976, *19* (6), 351-374.

Heider, F. *The Psychology of Interpersonal Relations.* New York: Wiley, 1958.

Kelley, H. H. "The Process of Causal Attribution." *American Psychologist,* 1973, *28,* 107-128.

Kohlberg, L. "The Study of Moral Development." In T. Likona (Ed.), *Moral Development and Behavior.* New York: Holt, Rinehart and Winston, 1976.

Kohlberg, L. "Stage and Sequence: The Cognitive-Developmental Approach to Socialization." In D. A. Goslin (Ed.), *Handbook of Socialization Theory and Research.* Chicago: Rand McNally, 1969.

Kuhn, D. "The Development of Role-Taking Ability." Unpublished manuscript, Columbia University, 1972.

Lavin, D. "A Study of the Patterns of Social Reasoning in Emotionally Disturbed Children Under Varying Contexts." Unpublished manuscript, Harvard-Judge Baker Social Reasoning Project, Harvard University, 1977.

Mead, G. H. *Mind, Self, and Society.* Chicago: University of Chicago Press, 1934.

Piaget, J. *The Origins of Intelligence in Children.* New York: International Universities Press, 1952.

Piaget, J. *The Moral Judgment of the Child.* New York: Harcourt Press, 1932.

Rest, J. "Developmental Psychology as a Guide to Value Education: A Review of Kohlbergian Programs." *Review of Educational Research,* 1974, *44,* 241-259.

Selman, R., and Jaquette, D. "Stability and Oscillation in Interpersonal Awareness: A Clinical-Developmental Approach. In C. B. Keasy (Ed.), *Nebraska Symposium on Motivation.* Vol. 25. Lincoln: University of Nebraska Press, forthcoming.

Selman, R., Jaquette, D., and Lavin, D. "Interpersonal Awareness in Children: Toward an Integration of Developmental and Clinical Child Psychology." *American Journal of Orthopsychiatry,* 1977, *47* (1), 264-274.

Selman, R., and Jaquette, D. "The Development of Interpersonal Awareness: A Working Draft Manual." Unpublished scoring manual, Harvard-Judge Baker Social Reasoning Project, Harvard University, 1977.

Selman, R. "Toward a Structural Analysis of Developing Interpersonal Relations Concepts: Research with Normal and Disturbed Preadolescent Boys." In A. Pick (Ed.), *X Annual Minnesota Symposium on Child Psychology.* Minneapolis: University of Minnesota Press, 1976.

Selman, R. "Social-Cognitive Understanding." In T. Lickona (Ed.), *Moral Development and Behavior.* New York: Holt, Rinehart and Winston, 1976a.

Selman, R., and Byrne, D. F. "A Structural-Developmental Analysis of Levels of Role-Taking in Middle Childhood." *Child Development,* 1974, *45,* 803-806.

Shaw, M., and Sulzer, J. "An Empirical Test of Heider's Levels in Attribution of Responsibility." *Journal of Abnormal and Social Psychology,* 1964, *69,* 39-46.

Turiel, E. "The Development of Social Concepts: Mores, Customs and Conventions." In D. J. DePalma and F. M. Foley (Eds.), *Moral Development: Current Theory and Research.* Hillsdale, N.J.: L. Erlbaum, 1975.

*Ellen Ward Cooney is assistant professor of psychology at Hampshire College, Amherst, Massachusetts. She received her masters and doctorate from Harvard University and completed a clinical internship in child psychology at the Judge Baker Guidance Center in Boston.*

*Robert L. Selman was until this year the director of the Manville School of the Judge Baker Guidance Center, and he now holds a Career Development Research Scientist award from the National Institute of Mental Health. Dr. Selman also lectures at the Harvard Graduate School of Education.*

*Children's social-cognitive development takes place
within certain domains: moral, societal,
and psychological. Judgments within each of these
domains guide the child's understanding
and use of social rules.*

# social regulations and domains of social concepts

## elliot turiel

From a relatively young age, children participate in social groups and
are involved in symbolic interactions with social systems. Consequently, it may be expected that through such interactions children
form concepts about social systems. Within social systems there exist
behavioral uniformities that constitute knowledge shared by individuals involved in ongoing interactions. Certain uniformities, which
may be termed *social conventions*, serve the function of coordinating
the actions of individuals within a social system. The development of
children's concepts of social conventions, therefore, is clearly related to
the development of children's concepts of social systems.

By proposing that social convention forms part of the individual's descriptive understanding of systems of social interactions, I am
differentiating social convention from moral prescriptions (Turiel,
1975). In this perspective, morality is defined not by coordination of
interactions within social organizations but by principles of justice prescriptive of behavior (Frankena, 1963; Rawls, 1971). However, the
proposed distinction between morality and social convention is one

usually not made in explanations of moral development (for example, Aronfreed, 1968; Hogan, 1973; Kohlberg, 1969; Piaget, 1932). It has generally been assumed that morality and convention are part of one domain and do not develop independently of each other. In contrast, I have proposed that social convention is part of a conceptual domain that is distinct from the moral domain. Concepts of social convention are part of the societal domain, which refers to concepts of social systems and social organizations (Turiel, forthcoming).

In fact, the distinction between the moral and societal domains is part of a more general model of social cognition (Turiel, forthcoming), in which it is maintained that concepts are organized *within* domains and not necessarily *across* domains. In this more general model, I distinguish between conceptual domains and methods of obtaining information about the social environment. The conceptual domains refer to the individual's ways of structuring or organizing the social environment. Three basic social conceptual domains are identified: the *moral* (justice), the *societal* (social groups, social organizations, and social systems), and the *psychological* (attributes of the person and causes of behavior). The methods of information gathering (for example, observation, communication, and role taking), which serve different cognitive functions from the conceptual frameworks, represent the activities by which informational aspects of the social environment are obtained.

This chapter is concerned with three general topics: social convention, morality, and social rules. I propose that, with regard to the development of social concepts, neither morality nor social convention can be adequately defined as rule-following behavior and that morality is distinct from social convention. The research discussed here deals with how children and adolescents understand the conventions of social systems and how they distinguish between social convention and morality.

## classification of social domains

A basic assumption of the structural approach to development is that human thought consists of systems of organization in which the elements or parts are subordinated to the laws of the whole (Piaget, 1970). Developmental changes stem from the individual's interactions with the environment and are reflected in progressive restructuring of systems of organization. Within this perspective, therefore, development refers to the individual's progress through a series of organized structures of thought and action, which are sequentially transformed through active ordering of experienced events. On this basis, several proponents of the structural-developmental approach have described stepwise changes in the organization of thought within a variety of domains (Damon, 1977; Inhelder and Piaget, 1958; Kohlberg, 1969; Langer, 1969; Piaget, 1970; Turiel, 1969).

Two different interpretations, global and partial, exist regarding systems of cognitive organization. The global interpretation maintains that all forms of thought are interrelated. Within the global interpretation, structure is defined as a unity or wholeness of cognitive activities. Thus, development is viewed as a process in which there are transformations of structural elements that are applicable across domains. Typically, it has been proposed that logical, physical, and social concepts are all structurally interrelated. In formulations of this proposition, globally defined stages of cognitive development combining both logical and physical concepts (as described by Piaget, 1966, 1970) are hypothesized to be the basis for the development of social concepts. One specific proposition, for instance, is that development within the cognitive stages is necessary but not sufficient for the development of corresponding stages or moral judgments (Keasey, 1975; Kohlberg, 1969, 1976; Kuhn and others, 1977; Selman, 1976b; Tomlinson-Keasey and Keasey, 1974).

The evidence provided in support of the proposed structural relations between different domains comes from correlational studies. However, correlations between different measures of developmental level do not provide an adequate means of testing the hypothesis of structural relations. At best, correlations provide an assessment of the degree of correspondence in (and patterns of) the *rates* of change of the two measures used. In other words, measures of two structurally unrelated aspects of conceptual development could produce high correlation coefficients if there were a correspondence in their individual rates of change. This is clearly demonstrated in a recently reported finding by Fisher (1977) of a high correlation (0.88) between a developmental sequence of classification skills in two- to seven-year-old children and their shoe size.

Consequently, since all the studies have been correlational, no evidence presently exists to support the hypothesis that logical, physical, and social concepts are structurally interrelated. In the course of this chapter, I will present evidence from noncorrelational studies on morality and social convention supporting the proposition that these constitute distinct conceptual domains. From the perspective of the partial-structure hypothesis, the assumption is that thought is organized (and changes sequentially) within a domain and not necessarily across domains. This has its basis in the constructivist and interactional propositions that conceptual knowledge is formed out of the child's actions upon the environment. To form concepts about objects and events, the child must act on them. The child's developing structures form the basis for interaction with the environment and represent a synthesis between thought, actions, and the structure of the environment. It follows, then, that the nature of conceptual constructions, though not determined by the environment, would be influenced by it. Therefore, interactions with fundamentally different types of objects and events should result in the production of different conceptual domains (see Turiel, 1975, 1978, for further elaboration).

In summary, it is proposed that individuals develop independent domains of knowledge. The assumption of independent structural systems implies that relations between these systems are of an informational nature rather than of interdependence. That is, independent systems may be coordinated with each other in the sense that one system provides information stimulating or facilitating change in another.

In this view, the child's interactions with the physical environment differ from those with the social world, and therefore physical concepts are distinct from social concepts (Turiel, 1975). Furthermore, as the distinction between social convention and morality implies, not all social knowledge is of one kind. Within this approach, therefore, a fundamental task is to identify the different domains of social knowledge.* A general classification of social domains emerges from a consideration of the types of social phenomena that are part of individual-

*The identification of the basic categories of social knowledge is necessary for a systematic understanding of social-cognitive development. Most frequently, researchers have chosen issues to study that are considered important in social life. On that basis, there have been studies of such issues as morality, friendship, authority, self, role-taking, presocial behavior and aggression. While such an issue-oriented approach can provide very useful information, nevertheless structural analyses require that specific issues be related to the broader categories of social knowledge—of which they form a part. However, an unfortunate consequence of the identification of specific issues, without concern for the classification of domains, is that historical precedence and availability have had an undue influence on theory and research. That is, those issues first studied tend to be treated as global structures that can be generalized to other social judgments.

environment interactions. In the first place, the child's social environment is composed of other individuals, and interactions with them produce knowledge about persons. However, social experiences are not limited to actions toward persons; the individual also interacts with patterns of social relations of descriptive and prescriptive kinds. These different social phenomena are the basis for my working model, in which three general categories of social concepts are identified. These include two classes of descriptive understanding—the psychological and societal—and one class of prescriptive understanding—the moral. The psychological domain refers to the child's developing concepts of the person (self and other), for example, causes and predictions of behavior, identity, and inferences about psychological attributes. The societal domain refers to the child's developing concepts of stable systems of interactions between persons, for example, groups, social organizations, and social structure. The moral domain refers to the child's developing concepts of justice and fairness.

Each of these general domains encompasses a variety of issues requiring investigation. Social convention is one central element in the coordination of social interactions within stable social systems and is thus part of the societal domain. As already stated, the research discussed here deals with the development of social conventional and moral concepts. The basis for distinguishing between morality and convention, however, needs to be clarified by first considering their definitions.

### morality, social convention, and social regulation

I am treating morality, social convention, and social regulation as three separate topics. It is often the case, however, that social convention is not distinguished from morality and that morality is defined as rule-following behavior. As an example, on the basis of the definition of morality as rule-following behavior, it would be assumed that people refrain from committing murder because they adhere to the rule that one should not kill. Moreover, the individual's conception of, or behavioral orientation toward, social rules is regarded as unitary; thus any form of rule-following behavior is classified within the moral domain. Piaget (1932), for instance, assumed that findings from his studies of children's conceptions of game rules could be generalized to their moral judgments.

The general premise that any type of rule can be used to study moral functioning is also accepted by social-learning theorists in their experiments on the internalization of moral behavior. In many such experiments the behavior measured is whether, or the extent to which, the child learns to adhere to a prohibition against playing with some toys in the experimental room (for example, pairs of toys are presented and the prohibition is against playing with the more attractive of each pair). One of the striking features of these experiments is that the action required of the child—to refrain from playing with a toy—is an arbitrary restriction established by the experimenter for the experimental situation. Without altering the moral status of the act, the experimenter could just as well establish a variety of restrictions regarding the toys. In these experiments, the implicit definition of moral behavior is adherence to prohibitions designated by the experimenter.

Within the definition of morality as rule-following behavior, it follows that game rules and prohibitions regarding toys would be classified in the same domain as rules regarding killing or theft. Similarly, rules such as those regarding modes of dress or sexual behavior would be considered part of the moral domain. However, the premises that individuals have a unitary concept of rules and that all rules are part of the same domain need to be questioned. Are rules pertaining to dress or sexual behavior, for instance, conceptualized in the same way as the rule that one should not kill?

In our culture at least, it is not the case that these different rules are conceptualized in the same way. One of the ways by which the different rules thus far mentioned can be distinguished from each other is on the basis of the type of action to which they pertain. Taking a life is a different type of action from sexual behavior (or wearing a certain mode of dress or playing with a toy), even if each action constitutes a violation of explicit regulations in the social system. Rules, therefore, are not of one kind in that they may vary according to the domain of the action involved. Indeed, a series of studies has shown that children and adolescents conceptualize rules that apply to the moral domain differently from rules that apply to the domain of social convention. Moreover, if it is the case that not all regulations are moral, then it would be incorrect to define morality (or conventions) as rule-following behavior. An alternative is the proposition that individuals have forms of thinking about morality, just as they have forms of thinking about the domains of the societal and the psychological. In other words, judgments within each of these domains guide the individual's understanding and use of rules.

As I have noted earlier, social conventions are behavioral uniformities that coordinate the actions of individuals participating in a social system. As such, conventions constitute shared knowledge of uniformities in social interactions. Examples of social conventional acts include uniformities in modes of dress, usages of forms of address (for example, first name or title plus last name), and modes of greeting. Social conventional acts are somewhat arbitrary in that they do not have an intrinsically prescriptive basis. Therefore, alternative courses of action can serve identical functions; that is, a conventional uniformity within one social unit may serve the same function as a different conventional uniformity in another social unit. Consider, for example, conventional uniformities regarding modes of dress. Typically, semiformal attire is worn in certain social contexts. The specific character of this conventional uniformity is arbitrary, and the content of this conventional uniformity is arbitrarily designated. Uniform modes of dress other than semiformal attire could just as well be designated as appropriate for the business office or church. Therefore, although social conventions often have a specifiable function within a given social context, their significance (unlike that of moral regulations) derives solely from that particular context.

The individual's concepts of social convention are, therefore, closely related to his or her concepts of social organization. The developmental proposition is that children form concepts of culture and social organization. That is to say, children develop a sociological orientation. The child's descriptive understanding of social organization needs to be distinguished from his or her moral prescriptions. I have defined morality as justice: "It is proposed that children develop concepts of justice which apply to a relatively limited range of issues, including the value of life, physical and psychological harm to others, trust, responsibility, etc. In contrast to convention, moral considerations stem from factors intrinsic to actions: consequences such as harm inflicted upon others, violation of rights, effects on the general welfare" (Turiel, forthcoming, pp. 5-6).

In the case of conventions, therefore, the specific content of the uniformity can be varied without altering the functions served; conventional uniformities are defined relative to the social-situational context. Accordingly, within the conventional domain, it is only violations of implicit or explicit regulations that can be considered transgressions. For an individual to regard a particular act as a transgression, he or she would have to possess culture-specific information about the act's status as a socially determined regularity. This is not the case in the moral domain. A social uniformity is not necessary for an individual to view an event as a moral transgression. In those cases (as an example, one child hitting another), the individual's perception of that event as a transgression stems from features intrinsic to the event (for example, from a perception of the consequences to the victim). Moral issues are neither arbitrary nor relative to the social context.

This difference in response to moral and social conventional transgressions was observed in children as young as four and five years of age. In a study by Nucci and Turiel (1978), preschool children were questioned about spontaneously occurring moral and social conventional transgressions (as reliably classified by our criteria) that they had observed. The children were asked whether an act would be wrong if there were no rule in the school pertaining to the act. When questioned about social conventional transgressions, in 81 percent of the cases the children stated that the act would be all right if no rule existed in the school. When questioned about moral transgressions, in 86 percent of the cases the children stated that the act would not be right even if no rule existed.

The Nucci and Turiel study also showed, as hypothesized earlier, that the types of social interactions experienced by young children do differ by domain. Using a response-category checklist to measure reactions to transgressions, it was found that when a child performed moral transgressions, others generally responded by giving the child feedback on the effects of the child's actions on others and on the emotional reactions of others; whereas when a child performed a social conventional transgression, others responded by giving the child feedback on aspects of the social order.

## concepts of social rules

I have said that rules may pertain to the moral domain and to the conventional domain and that the individual's conception of a rule is related to the domain of the action to which the rule pertains. In such a case, individuals would not possess a unitary concept of rules in that the meaning and function attributed to a given rule is dependent on its domain. Thus, it is to be expected that evaluation of rules about conventional acts would be based on their societal context, while evaluations of rules about moral acts would be based on factors intrinsic to the actions involved.

A series of studies has demonstrated that, indeed, concepts of social rules held by children and adolescents do vary in accordance with the domain of the rule. Moreover, it has been found that this distinction between moral and conventional rules is not age related. In the first of these studies, the subjects (eighty-six males and females, ranging from six to seventeen years of age) were posed a series of questions about specific rules. One set of questions dealt with rules pertaining to moral issues that existed in the subject's home and school, and game rules. The home, school, and game rules used in the inquiry had been generated by the subject. First, the subject was asked to list rules that existed in his or her home and school. The experimenter classified these rules as conventional or moral on the basis of previously determined criteria. The subject was asked questions about one conventional and one moral rule both within the home and within the school. The subject was also asked questions about a game rule that he or she had generated.

Subjects were also questioned about a series of rules presented to them. These rules pertained to the prohibition of stealing within the legal system (moral rules), the mode of dress in a business office (conventional rule), the use of titles in school (conventional rule), and the dress code in school (conventional rule).

For now, I can only present a partial analysis of the study based on subjects' rating of the importance of the rules and responses to questions dealing with the relativity of the rules. The importance of each rule was rated by subjects on a four-point scale, "1" being very important and "4" being not important. The perceived *relativity* of rules was assessed through questions about rules in a country different from the subject's own (for example, "Suppose there is another country in which there is no rule regarding X. Is that right?")

First, consider the findings from the importance ratings of the different rules. The average importance ratings given by subjects are as follows: stealing (legal system), 1.18; moral (school), 1.45; moral (home), 1.66; convention (school), 2.41; convention (home), 2.07; games, 2.38; dress in business office, 2.41; titles in school, 2.89; dress code in school, 2.97. These results indicate that the highest ratings were attributed to the moral rules, first stealing and then moral rules in the school and in the home. The conventional rules were given lower ratings than the moral rules. This pattern applies to the school and home rules generated by the subjects as well as to the rules presented to the subjects. Game rules were also given lower ratings of importance than the moral rules, receiving about the same rating as the conventional rules.

The differences between the ratings of moral rules and the ratings of conventional rules were statistically significant. Differences were found in the following comparisons: between moral school and conventional school rules ($F$ 1,75 = 72.5; $p<0.0001$); between moral home and conventional home rules ($F$ 1,64 = 56.69; $p<0.0001$); between moral home and school rules, grouped together, and conventional home and school rules, grouped together ($F$ 1,64 = 56.69; $p<0.0001$). In addition, the ratings of game rules were significantly different from the ratings of the stealing rules, of moral school rules, and of moral home rules ($F$ 1,70 = 107; $p<0.0001$). It was also found that there were no differences between the age groups studied. Subjects of different ages rated a given rule in similar ways, and no statistically significant age differences were found for any of the rules. Only the age differences on ratings of game rules were even marginally significant ($p = 0.09$).

It was also found that subjects' views of the relativity of rules were related to domain. The relevant results are in Table 1, which presents the percentage of subjects at each age who responded affirmatively or negatively to questions regarding the relativity and universality of the different rules. With regard to stealing, the majority of subjects at all ages stated that it would not be right for another country to have no rule prohibiting stealing. Similarly, the majority of subjects at all ages stated that it would not be right to steal in another country, even if there were no rule prohibiting stealing. In each case, the number of subjects responding in the negative was highly significantly different from chance expectancy. There were no significant age differences in the responses to either of these questions.

The results for the question regarding the relativity of moral home rules were more equivocal, however, than for the stealing rule. The majority of the youngest subjects stated that it would not be right if no families in another country had the rule, while the older subjects were more evenly split on this question (these age differences were marginally significant, $p = 0.07$).

The patterns of responses to questions about conventional home rules were clearly different from responses to questions about the stealing and moral home rules. The majority of subjects stated that it would be all right if no families in another country had the rule. There were no significant age differences for responses to this question. Fur-

## Table 1. Percentages of Subjects Responding Yes or No to Relativity Questions

| Type of Rule | Question | Response | AGE GROUPS | | | | | | All Ages |
|---|---|---|---|---|---|---|---|---|---|
| | | | 6-7 (n=16) | 8-9 (n=12) | 10-11 (n=13) | 12-13 (n=18) | 14-15 (n=14) | 16-17 (n=13) | (n=86) |
| Stealing | Suppose in another country there is no rule against stealing. Is it all right to have no rule? | Yes | 12 | 11 | 7 | 24 | 23 | 31 | 18 |
| | | No | 88 | 89 | 85 | 76 | 77 | 54 | 78 |
| | | Depends | – | – | 8 | – | – | 15 | 4 |
| | | | | | | | | Sign test: $p<0.0001$ | |
| Stealing | Suppose in another country there is no rule against stealing. Would it be all right to steal? | Yes | 15 | 30 | 25 | 6 | 0 | 15 | 14 |
| | | No | 85 | 70 | 75 | 94 | 100 | 77 | 85 |
| | | Depends | – | – | – | – | – | 8 | 1 |
| | | | | | | | | Sign test: $p<0.0001$ | |
| Moral Home | Suppose there is another country in which no families have that rule. Is that all right? | Yes | 19 | 67 | 67 | 54 | 33 | 50 | 45 |
| | | No | 81 | 22 | 33 | 31 | 42 | 50 | 46 |
| | | Depends | – | 11 | – | 15 | 25 | – | 9 |
| | | | | | | | | Sign test: n.s. | |
| Conventional Home | Suppose there is another country in which no families have that rule. Is that all right? | Yes | 40 | 91 | 86 | 86 | 70 | 82 | 73 |
| | | No | 60 | 9 | 14 | 14 | 15 | 18 | 23 |
| | | Depends | – | – | – | – | 15 | – | 4 |
| | | | | | | | | Sign test: $p<0.001$ | |
| Game | Suppose that everybody in another country decided to play by different rules. Would that be all right? | Yes | 100 | 83 | 83 | 94 | 92 | 100 | 90 |
| | | No | 0 | 17 | 17 | 6 | 8 | 0 | 10 |
| | | | | | | | | Sign test: $p<0.001$ | |

All sign tests refer to the null hypothesis that the proportions of subjects responding yes or no are equal.

thermore, there were statistically significant differences on the relativity questions between responses to the moral rules and responses to the conventional rules.

Finally, the patterns of responses to the game rules were similar to responses to the conventional rules. These findings show that Piaget's (1932) generalization of children's concepts of game rules to their concepts of moral rules was invalid. The majority of subjects at all ages stated that it would be all right for everybody in a different country to play the game by different rules.

The combined findings that subjects attributed greater importance to moral than to conventional rules and that conventional rules were viewed relative to the social context are open to two interpretations. One interpretation is that a subject's views on the relativity of rules, whether in the moral or conventional domain, are based on the importance attributed to the rules. A second interpretation, more consistent with my domain analysis, is that a subject's views on the relativity of rules reflect the ways in which he or she conceptualizes the conventional and moral domains and that the importance attributed to the rules stems from those conceptualizations.

The finding that there were no age differences in the importance ratings suggests that the second interpretation is correct. If the differences in attribution of importance did not stem from a systematic conceptual source, then it is likely that there sould be more variability in the importance ratings of subjects of different ages. In other words, six- and sixteen-year-olds, for example, are likely to vary in the rules that they consider important unless there is a commonality in the way that they conceptually discriminate between the different types of rules.

Furthermore, a study by Nucci (1977) provides more direct evidence for the domain interpretation of the importance ratings. Nucci presented subjects (ages seven to nineteen years) with a series of statements (or cartoon strips for the younger subjects) depicting actors engaging in moral or social conventional transgressions. (Nucci also included a third category that he labeled "personal," which is not germane to the present discussion). Subjects were first asked to sort the statements into three categories on the basis of the statements' degree of wrongness. In accordance with the findings of the Turiel study, subjects of all ages considered the moral transgressions as being "more wrong" than the conventional transgressions. These subjects were also interviewed about their reasons for sorting the transgressions as they had. Indeed, the reasons given for classifying moral transgressions as "more wrong" were of a different type than were the reasons for classifying conventional transgressions as "less wrong." The moral transgressions were classified because of considerations of fairness, injustice, and the consequences to others; the classification of conventional transgressions was based on considerations of rules, authority, and social order or disorder.

An additional finding from the Nucci study was consistent with the results of the Turiel and the Nucci and Turiel studies. Subjects were also asked to select those statements describing acts that they considered "wrong regardless of the absence of a rule." Subjects selected almost all the statements depicting moral transgressions and very few of the statements depicting social conventional transgressions. Using different methods, this finding has been replicated in a study by D. Weston and myself. Two hypothetical situations, in story form, were presented to subjects (ages five, seven, nine, and eleven years). One story, which dealt with an act in the moral domain, described a school in which children were allowed to hit (and hurt) each other. A second story, dealing with a social conventional act, described a school in which children were allowed to be without any clothes. In each case subjects were asked (1) whether it was all right for the school to allow the act and (2) to evaluate the act of a child who engaged in the action (that is, hitting another child or removing one's clothing).

The findings were consistent with our expectations. The majority of subjects in each age group stated that it was not all right for the school to permit hitting and that it would be wrong for a child to adhere to that policy. In contrast, most subjects stated that it would be all right for a school to permit children to remove their clothes and for a child to adhere to that policy.

Taken together, the results from all the studies reviewed support the proposition that concepts of rules vary according to domain. Rules pertaining to moral events are not viewed as relative to social settings because they are evaluated on the basis of factors intrinsic to the regulated act. Thus, judgments and evaluations about a given rule would correspond to judgments and evaluations of the act to which it pertains. If an act is intrinsically valued, then a rule pertaining to the act would be viewed as unchangeable and universally desirable. In contrast, rules pertaining to conventional events are viewed as relative to a given social setting, because the regulated acts are themselves evaluated as arbitrary. Such acts function to coordinate social interactions within a social system.

These results, therefore, have a bearing on the previously men-

social organization (see Turiel, 1978, for further discussion).

tioned "forbidden-toy" experiments, as well as on the internalization theory from which they stem (Aronfreed, 1968; Grinder, 1962; Hogan, 1973; Sears, Rau, and Alpert, 1965). It will be recalled that in those experiments the subject was presented with an arbitrary restriction—to refrain from playing with a designated toy. The experiments were based on the assumption that moral behaviors are merely arbitrary acts that become behaviorally nonarbitrary for the individual through the appropriate psychological manipulations. That is, a moral behavior is any behavior conditioned or internalized through rewards and punishments. Of course, any such learned moral behavior can just as well be made arbitrary again through its deconditioning (extinction).

Classifying the learning of arbitrary acts as moral learning is consistent with the internalization view that morality is convention, convention being defined as conformity to external norms. For this reason, morality has been defined by consensus. As an example, moral values have been defined as "evaluations of actions generally believed by the members of a given society to be either 'right' or 'wrong.' . . . A person has strong moral values if he shares in the cultural consensus" (Berkowitz, 1964, p. 44). However, the findings that I have discussed indicate instead that the cognitive basis for conventional rules differs from that for moral rules.

All the studies reviewed here have also shown that the distinction between moral and conventional rules is made across a wide age range. These findings provide evidence from *noncorrelational* studies that social convention and morality constitute distinct conceptual domains. This evidence also has a bearing on previous structural-developmental explanations (Kohlberg, 1969, 1976; Piaget, 1932) of moral judgment. Both Piaget and Kohlberg have presented stage models of moral-judgment development in which it is assumed that moral reasoning emerges from separating moral from nonmoral processes. In their formulations, less developed moral systems are based on conformity to conventionally defined rules, while more advanced systems are based on principles distinct from conventional rules. Consequently, social convention is treated as part of *moral* development and relegated to early developmental states. That is, it is assumed that development progresses from a state of conformity to the conventions of the social system to a state of autonomous and principled moral reasoning. The most advanced forms of moral judgment are defined as ones in which concepts of justice *displace* concepts of convention and social organization (see Turiel, 1978, for further discussion).

I have proposed an alternative view of social convention. Convention is part of the individual's conceptualization of nonmoral aspects of the social interaction and develops alongside the development of justice concepts. Thus, convention represents one of the ways in which individuals conceptually construct their understanding of the social environment. The research presented thus far shows that morality and convention are distinguished by subjects ranging from four to nineteen years of age. Other research, to which I now turn, has focused directly on the form and development of social conventional concepts.

## concepts of social convention

The research into children's concepts of rules indicates that the distinction between the moral and conventional domains represents a nondevelopmental dimension. In contrast, research into children's concepts of social convention has shown that these concepts *are* age related. In this research, what has been termed the clinical method*

---

*The theoretical rationale and empirical criteria for the clinical method have been extensively discussed (Damon, 1977; Kohlberg, 1966, 1969; Turiel, 1969; Werner, 1957). In spite of the availability of these discussions of the clinical method, findings from its use have been incorrectly evaluated in accordance with methodological criteria taken directly from the alternative method of standardized testing (i.e., the method used in I.Q. tests and most personality tests). A blatant example of this type of evaluation can be seen in a critical review by Kurtines and Greif (1974) of Kohlberg's (1963, 1969) methods of studying the development of moral judgments.

The clinical interview method is designed to obtain information about the form of reasoning, rather than just the conclusions or attitudes held (content). Such interviews contain questions aimed at stimulating the subject to explain the basis for his conclusions as fully as possible. Accordingly, the interviewer probes in such a way as to obtain the type of information adequate to an analysis of the organization of thought. In contrast with the clinical method, standardized tests are designed to elicit answers from the subject (such as an answer to an arithmetical problem), without analysis of the form of reasoning that produced the answer. Again unlike the clinical method, standardized tests yield a score reflecting a quantitative assessment of the testee's capacity or trait (such as an I.Q. score). The clinical method was originally developed by Piaget (1928) as an alternative to standardized testing. Piaget had concluded that standardized tests did not yield sufficient information regarding the reasoning used by the child to arrive at his answers and that, therefore, the study of intelligence required different procedures.

Clearly, the differences in theoretical assumptions and methodological criteria between the clinical method and standardized tests are fundamental ones. Nevertheless, these differences are not always understood. Kurtines and Greif (1974) used criteria derived from standardized testing to evaluate existing data from Kohlberg's structural theory (which are data obtained through the clinical method). There are many problems in the Kurtines and Greif analysis (see Broughton, 1975), including a

(Piaget, 1928) was used with 110 subjects ranging from six to twenty-five years of age. They were administered an interview that revolved around a series of hypothetical stories. Each of these stories dealt with a form of conventional usage about which subjects were extensively probed. The stories dealt with forms of address (a boy who wants to call teachers in school by their first names), modes of dress (dressing casually in a business office), sex-associated occupations (a boy who wants to become a nurse caring for infants when he grows up), patterns of family living arrangements in different cultures (fathers living apart from the rest of their families), and modes of eating (with hands or with knife and fork). A concrete example of the type of story used in the interview is a situation dealing with forms of address. The story concerns a boy, brought up by his parents to call people by their first names, who is expected to address teachers in his new school by their formal titles. He comes into conflict with the teachers and principal, who insist that he use titles and last names rather than first names.

Through analyses of subjects' responses to the interview questions, seven levels of social conventional concepts were identified. A summary of each of the seven levels is presented in Table 2. The levels represent age-related changes that can be reliably assessed in subjects' interview responses.

The seven levels identified support the proposition that social convention is a conceptual and developmental system. These levels show that the individual's understanding of convention is related to his or her concepts of social organization. Development progresses toward viewing conventions as shared knowledge of uniformities in social interactions within social systems and viewing such uniformities as functional in coordinating social interactions. However, conventions are

---

sloppy and selective use of data, as well as misunderstandings of elementary statistical procedures (for instance, they provided an inaccurate characterization of results from one of my studies because they failed to recognize the difference between a student *t* test and a Dunnett *t* test). However, the point I wish to make for the present purposes is that it is not scientifically legitimate to evaluate data from one methodology with criteria from an alternative methodology. I do *not* mean to say that it is not legitimate to debate the relative merits of the criteria of one approach over those of another. However, it is invalid to accept the tenets of one approach as if they were absolute and mechanically apply them to another (contrasting) approach. Therefore, the type of analysis done by Kurtines and Greif provides no basis for negatively or positively evaluating data generated by the clinical method. It is unfortunate that others (e.g., Elkind and Weiner, 1978; Evans and McCandless, 1978; Hoffman, 1977) have uncritically accepted the type of enterprise engaged in by Kurtines and Greif.

### Table 2. Major Changes in Social-Conventional Concepts

| | *Approximate Ages* |
|---|---|
| 1. *Convention as descriptive of social uniformity.* Convention viewed as descriptive of uniformities in behavior. Convention is not conceived as part of structure or function of social interaction. Conventional uniformities are descriptive of what is assumed to exist. Convention maintained to avoid violation of empirical uniformities. | 6-7 |
| 2. *Negation of convention as descriptive social uniformity.* Empirical uniformity not a sufficient basis for maintaining conventions. Conventional acts regarded as arbitrary. Convention is not conceived as part of structure or function of social interaction. | 8-9 |
| 3. *Convention as affirmation of rule system; early concrete conception of social system.* Convention seen as arbitrary and changeable. Adherence to convention based on concrete rules and authoritative expectations. Conception of conventional acts not coordinated with conception of rule. | 10-11 |
| 4. *Negation of convention as part of rule system.* Convention now seen as arbitrary and changeable regardless of rule. Evaluation of rule pertaining to conventional act is coordinated with evaluation of the act. Conventions are "nothing but" social expectations. | 12-13 |
| 5. *Convention as mediated by social system.* The emergence of systematic concepts of social structure. Convention as normative regulation in system with uniformity, fixed roles, and static hierarchical organization. | 14-16 |
| 6. *Negation of convention as societal standards.* Convention regarded as codified societal standards. Uniformity in convention is not considered to serve the function of maintaining social system. Conventions are "nothing but" societal standards that exist through habitual use. | 17-18 |
| 7. *Convention as coordination of social interactions.* Conventions as uniformities that are functional in coordinating social interactions. Shared knowledge, in the form of conventions, among members of social groups facilitates interaction and operation of the system. | 19-25 |

conceived to be, in some sense, arbitrary and related to the social system. The levels reflect changes in the connections between convention and the social system.

The seven levels also show that the process of development is one in which there is a series of oscillations between *affirmation* and *negation* of convention and social structure. Each affirmation entails a construction of concepts of conventions and social structure. Each phase of affirmation is followed by a phase negating the validity of the previous affirmative phase. In turn, each phase of negation leads to a new construction of convention and social structure. I should stress that the negation phases are not merely defined by the rejection of conventions; specific conventions may be rejected at affirmation phases as well. Furthermore, negation phases do not necessarily involve a total rejection of conventions. During negation phases, conventions may be adhered to for pragmatic or prudential reasons (for example, to avoid punishment). It is the reevaluation of the individual's concepts of social structure, as well as the conceived role of convention in social structure, that defines a negation phase.

Elsewhere I have described each of the levels of social conventional concepts in some detail and have provided examples of responses corresponding to each level (Turiel, 1978). The present discussion focuses on the two above-mentioned features of the findings: that the individual's understanding of convention is related to his or her concepts of social organization and that developmental changes involve conceptual reorganizations. As is outlined in Table 2, at level 1 the child's concepts of social organization are restricted to a recognition of uniformities in social behavior. Conventional uniformities are descriptive of what exists in the social world. At level 3 there is a concrete conception of social organization based on the functions of rules and authority. At level 5 there is an abstract concept of hierarchical systems of social organization. The level 5 conception is further elaborated into a level 7 view of conventions as serving the function of coordinating interactions through shared knowledge.

I will elaborate on this progression by contrasting the phases of affirmation and negation with each other. First, consider responses made by two subjects, one a six-year-old at level 1 and the other an eight-year-old at level 2. These subjects responded to a story that dealt with a young boy who wants to become a nurse caring for infants when he grows up, but his father thinks that he should not do so.

Level 1:

Joan (6 years, 5 months): (Should he become a nurse?) *Well, no, because he could easily be a doctor and he could take care of babies in the hospital.* (Why shouldn't he be a nurse?) *Well, because a nurse is a lady and the boys, the other men would just laugh at them.* (Why shouldn't a man be a nurse?) *Well, because it would be sort of silly because ladies wears those kind of dresses and those kind of shoes and hats.* (What is the difference between doctors and nurses?) *Doctors take care of them most and nurses just hand them things.* (Do you think his father was right?) *Yes, because, well, a nurse, she typewrites and stuff and all that.* (The man should not do that?) *No, because he would look silly in a dress.*

Level 2:
Susan (8 years, 6 months): *Right, because it doesn't matter. There are men nurses in the hospitals.* (What if there were not any in Joe's time, do you still think he should have done it?) *Yes, it doesn't matter if it is a man or woman it is just your job taking care of little children.* (Why do you think his parents think he should not take care of little kids?) *Because his father might be old-fashioned and he would think that men could not take care of babies.* (Why do you think he thinks that?) *Because it is a lady's job, because ladies know what babies are because they have them.* (You don't think that is true?) *No. Because ladies are the same and men might know a lot about babies too.*

The first level represents an affirmation phase, in which thinking about social conventions is featured by assumptions made regarding social uniformities. Social convention relates to these children's thinking through the meaning attributed to uniformities in behavior. Uniformities in social behavior are not understood to be means for coordinating social interactions or parts of a social system. Rather, uniformities are descriptive of behaviors and on that basis are interpreted as necessary and requiring conservation. As Joan's responses indicate, children at level 1 view certain occupations as necessarily associated with the class of male or female. Similarly, for children at this level titles are necessarily associated with classes of people (for example, child and adult). Correspondingly, observed behaviors or physical traits of classes of persons are interpreted as fixed and necessary of individuals within a classification. In considering whether a male could become a nurse, for example, Joan maintained that two types of (non-desirable) violations of uniformity would result if a male became a nurse: type of activity and type of dress. Thus conventions are seen as uniformities based on empirical regularities and not as forms of shared knowledge within a social system. Insofar as there is a conception of social structure at this level, it is based on perceived status distinctions that stem from empirical uniformities.

In contrast with Joan's responses, eight-year-old Susan does not regard the empirical associations of activities, roles, or labels (such as titles) with classes of persons as if they were necessary. At the second level, the negation of convention is based on the view that empirical uniformity is not a sufficient basis for judging behaviors as necessary, fixed, or requiring conservation. However, it is not merely the awareness of variations in behavior that distinguishes level 2 from level 1; more importantly, it is how such perceived differences are interpreted. For children at level 2, uniformity, even when it exists, does not imply necessity. In fact, it is asserted by those children that empirical associations of behaviors with classes of persons can lead other people to assume falsely that the behaviors are fixed and necessary. Two eight-year-olds put it as follows:

> Emily (8 years, 11 months): (Why do you think his parents see that job as for women only?) *Being a nurse—because not many men are nurses so they get used to the routine. I know a lot of ladies who are doctors, but I don't know a man who is a nurse, but it is okay if they want to.*

> John (8 years, 2 months): (Why do you think his parents see that job as for women only?) *Because most women do it. But on my baseball team there is a girl. So you can't say he can't. She is a good player in fact.*

A salient feature of social conventional thinking at level 2 is that the acts are regarded as arbitrary. On the basis of the assertion of the arbitrariness of these actions, subjects at the second level negate the necessity for convention. However, there is no awareness of the coordinative functions of convention, except as they concern the need to determine another's specific preferences. It is at level 3 that social convention is first conceptualized as an aspect of the social system. The basic change at this level is the emergence of concrete conceptions of social structure. Social conventional acts are evaluated in relation to rules, authoritative expectations, and maintenance of social order. First, consider the following responses, from two subjects to questions about forms of address. The first subject represents level 3, while the second subject represents the subsequent negation phase (level 4).

Level 3:
Bruce (11 years): (Do you think Peter was right or wrong to continue calling his teachers by their first names?) *Wrong, because the principal told him not to. Because it was a rule. It was one of the rules of the school.* (And why does that make it wrong to call a teacher by his first name?) *Because you should follow the rules.* (Do you think if there weren't a rule, that it would be wrong—or would it be right to call teachers by their first names?) *Right. Because if there wasn't a rule, it wouldn't matter. . . . It wouldn't matter what they called her if there wasn't a rule.*

Level 4:
Robert (12 years, 11 months): *Well, all the teachers were strict, right, and felt that he should call them sir, or mister. Well if I were a teacher, I don't think it should bother a teacher that he be called by his first name, but the way it is now, you really can't. But Peter actually should not have done it, because he could get himself into trouble, but I guess he could because that was the way he had been brought up and that was the way he thought it should be done.* (Why do you think he should not break the rule?) *He shouldn't break the rule? Because he could get into trouble for it and if you have to go to school you might as well not make it harder for yourself.* (What if Peter really believed that the rule was wrong? Do you think then it would be right or wrong for him to break a rule?) *Well, still, it is actually not wrong, because it is not going to make any difference because like I said before, maybe it is right for him to do it, but he would be getting himself into trouble if he did it.*

At level 3, conventions are regarded as contingent upon their social context: Rules and authoritative expectations require adherence to the conventions. Social relations are now seen as governed by a system in which individuals hold positions of authority, such as principals or teachers in a school or employers in a business firm. Nevertheless, subjects at level 3 regard social conventional acts as arbitrary, in the sense that it is assumed there is no intrinsic basis for the action. Apart from concrete rules or specific demands for compliance from authorities, conventional acts are not seen as necessary. In the absence of rules or authoritative expectations, conventions like forms of address, modes of dress, or manner of eating "do not matter." Rules pertaining to conventions (that is, acts otherwise regarded as arbitrary) are viewed as requiring adherence. Furthermore, it is assumed that the demands of authority or existing rules may vary from one social context to another.

Additionally, rudimentary notions of social order emerge at this level. It is assumed that maintenance of an existing social order is based on conformity to rules and authoritative expectations. For subjects at this level, therefore, the evaluation of what are regarded as arbitrary conventional acts depends on whether a rules exists. This means that the subject's conception of convention is not coordinated with his or her conception of rules or social context. That is, the rule is treated as obligatory and invariable, even though it pertains to an act that is otherwise treated as variable.

At level 4, rules and action are coordinated and there is a concomitant negation of convention. At this level the basic conception of conventional acts as arbitrary is maintained, as was the case with subjects at the previous two levels. Unlike subjects at level 3, however, subjects at level 4 coordinate their evaluation of an act with the evaluation of the rule or expectation to which the act pertains. Given that conventional acts are viewed as arbitrary, it is maintained by these subjects that rules or expectations about such acts are not valid. For instance, the use of titles is regarded as arbitrary. It is the ability to communicate with others that these subjects regard as important. As was stated by Robert, names are ways of identifying people, and communication can be achieved via the use of first names or titles. Therefore, the negation of convention at this level is different from the level 2 negation, which is based on a rejection of the idea that uniformity implies necessity. Subjects at levels 3 and 4 would also reject this idea. But the negation at level 4 involves an evaluation of rules and authoritative expectations on the basis of the acts to which they pertain.

The change from the third to the fourth level in the conception of rules pertaining to conventional acts results in the view that conventions are *nothing but* the expectations of others. This orientation stems from an awareness that, indeed, expectations do exist regarding what appear to these subjects as arbitrary acts. Consequently, social expectations are rejected as an insufficient basis for regulation of behavior.

Through the level 4 process of negating convention and questioning the level 3 concept of social structure, the adolescent remains without a systematic understanding of the organization of social interactions. At level 5, adolescents construct systematic concepts of social organization. Notions are now formed about individuals as part of more general social units or as part of a collective system. Social structure is now defined not by rules and authority (as is the case at level 3) but as a system of organization for the social interactions of its members. At level 5, convention is defined as shared behavior mediated by common concepts of society. Normative characteristics are viewed as central to social units. Conventionally shared behavior is necessary because of the function served by uniformity in the social system. At this fifth level, therefore, convention is viewed as normative regulation in a system with uniformity, fixed roles, and static hierarchical organization.

There are two distinguishable phases at the fifth level. During the first phase, uniformity is a defining characteristic of a collectivity: Adherence to conventional uniformities is necessary for participation in the collectivity. In the second phase, uniformity represents a general consensus that is codified and that functions to maintain the social order. During the first phase, social acts are judged in relation to a group or social system in which the individual is subordinate. For these subjects, the individual's adherence to uniformities is a necessary accommodation to the group in order to be a participant. Participation in group or collective life is not considered an obligation for the individual. However, if an individual is part of the group, then adherence to its uniformities is necessary. Deviance from conventional behavior is a violation of the legitimate expectations of others who are part of the group. In the following example, it can be seen how uniformity is related to the social system:

> Richard (17 years, 1 month): (Do you think Peter was right or wrong to continue calling his teachers by their first names?) *I think he was wrong, because you have to realize that you should have respect for your elders and that respect is shown by addressing them by their last names.* (Why do you think that shows respect?) *Informally, you just call any of your friends by their first names, but you really don't have that relation with a teacher. Whereas with parents too, you call them Mom and Dad and it's a different relation than the other two.* (What if Peter thought it didn't make any difference what you called

called people, that you could still respect them no matter what you called them?) *I think he'd have to realize that you have to go along with the ways of other people in your society.*

In the second phase of this level, there is an extension of the conception of social systems, which then leads to the next negation (level 6). In the first phase of level 5, uniformity in conventions is related to group participation; in the second phase, it is also assumed that conventional uniformities in social groups, particularly at the societal level, are necessary for maintenance of society. Conventions are codified, and they represent common or shared knowledge on the part of the members of a social system. The following responses illustrate level 5 thinking and its level 6 negation:

Level 5:
James (15 years, 11 months): *I think he's wrong, because in his family he can call his mother and father by their first names. But when he's in public he's got to respect the rules of the school. (*Why does he have to respect the rules of the school?) *How can you be one individual? If everyone else—he's one individual and his family is brought up with first names. In school, it's a rule to call people by their last names, and if it's a rule he can't be the only one who's not going to do it. He's just going to have to live with it. Even if his family taught him like that, he doesn't have to tell them . . . he cannot do it. It's just the principle of the thing. Because it's different if a lot of families did it, but I think he probably is just one exception. And he should obey the rules of the school.*

Brian (18 years, 8 months): *I think he was wrong because when he finds himself in school and everybody else calls the teacher Mr. or Mrs. or Miss, or whatever else it might be, he places himself in a position which is unfair to the other students; he establishes sort of personal relationships with the teachers by calling them by their first names and the other students might take it as an offense. (*Would that make it wrong?) *I think it would make him superior in the other students' eyes, or he would think he was superior and it would upset the balance that the class had.*

Level 6:

Kevin (17 years, 10 months): (Do you think Peter was right or wrong to continue calling his teachers by their first names?) *Well, obviously he was right. Just the fact that teachers in schools have to be called Mr. and Mrs. is no valid reason for that. And also they simply refuse to acknowledge the fact that he's used to calling people by their first names, which is a natural thing to do.* (Why is there no valid reason for calling teachers by. . . .) *Well, first there is no good reason for it, the reason is to give the teacher in the classroom respect and give him a feeling of power and authority over the kids in the class.*

Steve (19 years, 9 months): *Yah, he was right. The fault is with society in general because people like hierarchies for their own egos and part of that is having the old title, whatever it is. I think it is kind of unnecessary.*

At level 5, conventions are determined by general acceptance and are thereby binding on all members. Furthermore, the nature of relations between members of a social group are determined by social organization. For instance, the relation between student and teacher is determined by the social context of the school. Within the school context, the use of titles represents a uniform means for signifying the student-teacher relation. Having formed systematic concepts of social organization, subjects at the fifth level now define society as hierarchically ordered. Individuals are thereby classified on the basis of their role and status within the system. Conventions symbolize both roles and status. Status distinctions place constraints upon relationships, such that interactions between individuals of unequal status require conventional usages (for example, forms of address). In this sense, conventions are seen to regulate those relations between individuals that are determined by social organization.

At level 6, the function of convention is questioned. Conventions are still regarded as part of the social system and defined as codified societal standards (thus, level 6 negation differs from that of level 4). However, uniformity is no longer regarded as a necessary condition for the adequate functioning of social systems. Diversity or variation in the behavior of individuals is seen as compatible with the organization of a social system. Without the uniformity requirement, conventions are regarded as arbitrary dictates. The negation of level 6 is based on the premise that conventional uniformities are not necessary for the maintenance of a social system.

Level 7 is marked by a conception of conventions as necessary for the coordination of people's interactions in a more or less stable group relationship (for example, in a school, business firm, or society). The basic function of convention is to coordinate interactions between individuals and to integrate different parts of the social system. Conventional acts are regarded as arbitrary in that there is no principle intrinsic to acting in a particular way. Alternative (and perhaps opposing) courses of action may be equally valid. However, conventionally uniform or specified courses of action on the part of members of the social system are generally known, agreed-on modes of behavior (shared norms). The purpose of these uniformities is to coordinate interactions and thereby to facilitate the operation of a social system. As one nineteen-year-old put it:

> *Conventions make things move along smoothly and . . . are most consistently understandable communication. . . . If you communicate with somebody about something, you probably have some conventional way of talking about the thing you want to communicate, and the person you are trying to communicate to is also familiar with the general way of communicating this convention. Therefore he is able to follow you more quickly because he automatically is familiar with the way you start to do something, if it is the conventional way of doing something. So he doesn't have to stop and think how is that working, how is this thing said, because he has already been familiar with it. It shortens the process in many cases.*

For subjects at level 7, convention is based on common or shared knowledge and its primary function is to facilitate social interactions. Violations of conventions produce the inconveniences stemming from the failure to coordinate interactions or to maintain a social organization. When relying on conventions, each participant assumes a common understanding based on past experiences in similar situations. At the seventh level, conventional acts are clearly regarded as arbitrary. At the same time, conventions are viewed as serving the function of coordinating social interactions. These two features of social conventional concepts are characteristic of each of the seven levels, but they take different forms at each level. Conceptions of the arbitrary quality of social conventional acts and of their connections to social structure vary from level to level. Therefore, the developmental changes reflected in the progression through the seven levels also show that the individual's understanding of convention stems from his or her concepts of social systems.

As we have seen, however, the development of these societal conceptions proceeds through a series of oscillations between the affirmation and negation of convention. The observed patterns of oscillation suggest the developmental hypothesis that a negation phase is necessary for each new construction of concepts of social structure. This implies that development is a continual dialectical process in which the reevaluation of existing concepts of social structure prepares the way for the construction of new concepts.

## conclusions

The findings presented here support the proposition that social convention is part of the societal domain, which is distinct from the moral domain. Direct and noncorrelational evidence for this proposition comes from the studies of children's and adolescents' understanding of social rules within different domains.

The proposition of distinct conceptual domains has methodological implications for research on social development. Just as the individual's concepts may be classified according to domain, so can events. In the Nucci and Turiel (1978) study, it was found that spontaneously occurring social events could be reliably classified for domain and that children conceptualized events identified as social conventional differently from events identified as moral. These findings show that individuals conceptualize different types of social events in different ways. Therefore, in researching the development of social concepts, it is necessary to classify events or stimuli used.

I have maintained that most theories of moral development have failed to distinguish between social convention and morality. If this is correct, it would follow that there has been a failure to make the corresponding distinction in the stimuli used to elicit responses from subjects. Indeed, an extensive review of moral development research (Turiel, 1978) has shown that many of the stimulus events used in that research do not fall within the moral domain.

Two previously mentioned examples illustrate the ways in

*meaning + function of game rules distinguished from thise attributed to moral rules.*

which stimulus events have been used inappropriately in the study of moral development. The first example is the assessment of children's concepts of game rules as a means of assessing level of moral judgment (Piaget, 1932). The research findings have shown that children conceptually distinguish between game rules and rules pertaining to moral issues. Apparently, the meaning and function attributed to game rules by children is different from the meaning and function attributed to moral rules. Consequently, the use of game rules is not an appropriate methodology for the study of moral development (see Turiel, 1978 for further discussion).

A second example of a stimulus event frequently used to study moral development, but which should not be classified within the moral domain, is the measure of children's behavioral responses to a prohibition against playing with designated toys (the forbidden-toy paradigm). The effects of a number of variables on the internalization of the (presumed) moral prohibition have been studied through forbidden-toy experiments. These have included nurturance (Parke, 1967; Parke and Walters, 1967), modeling (Slaby and Parke, 1971; Walters, Parke, and Cane, 1965), intensity and timing of punishment (Aronfreed and Reber, 1965; Parke and Walters, 1967; Walters, Parke, and Cane, 1965), and verbal instructions (Cheyne, 1971; Cheyne, Goyeche, and Walters, 1969). From the viewpoint of the convention-morality distinction, however, the forbidden-toy paradigm would not be classified as a moral situation because the prohibition is an arbitrary restriction established by the experimenter for the experimental situation. As discussed earlier, the restrictions placed on the subjects are related solely to the scientific aims of the experiment: how the subject responds to a prohibition when there is presumably some temptation to violate it. Given the arbitrary (nonmoral) nature of the restriction imposed, it is likely that subjects would view the restriction as a rule or convention specific to the social interactions of the experimental situation. Indeed, the results of a number of studies using the forbidden-toy paradigm can be readily interpreted (see Turiel, 1978) as demonstrating that subjects behave in accordance with the perceived rules of the experimental situation.

These two stimulus events (game rules and the forbidden-toy paradigm) provide examples of the types of nonmoral situations that have been used to study moral concepts and behaviors. An adequate understanding of the individual's social development requires both delineation of domains of social concepts and specification of the domain of social events. When faced with a social stimulus, the subject's response is in part determined by the nature of the event. Generally the individual applies social conventional concepts to certain types of events, and moral concepts to other types of events. The use of stimuli that do not correspond to the conceptual domain under investigation is likely to produce inaccurate results. Consequently, the choice of stimulus events in research should be based on criteria (Turiel, 1978) that assure their appropriateness to the domain of the social concept or behavior under investigation.

## references

Aronfreed, J. *Conduct and Conscience: The Socialization of Internalized Control over Behavior.* New York: Academic Press, 1968.

Aronfreed, J., and Reber, A. "Internalized Behavioral Suppression and the Timing of Social Punishment." *Journal of Personality and Social Psychology,* 1965, *1,* 3-16.

Berkowitz, L. *Development of Motives and Values in the Child.* New York: Macmillan, 1964.

Broughton, J. M. "The Development of Natural Epistemology in the Years 10-26." Unpublished doctoral dissertation, Harvard University, 1975.

Cheyne, J. A. "Some Parameters of Punishment Affecting Resistance to Deviation and Generalization of a Prohibition." *Child Development,* 1971, *42,* 1249-1261.

Cheyne, J. A., Goyeche, J. R. M., and Walters, R. H. "Attention, Anxiety and Rules in Resistance to Deviation in Children." *Journal of Experimental Child Psychology,* 1969, *8,* 127-139.

Damon, W. *The Social World of the Child.* San Francisco: Jossey-Bass, 1977.

Elkind, D., and Weiner, I. B. *Development of the Child.* New York: John Wiley and Sons, 1978.

Evans, E. D., and McCandless, B. R. *Children and Youth.* New York: Holt, 1978.

Fisher, K. W. "Sequence and Synchrony in Cognitive Development." Symposium presented at the annual meeting of the American Psychological Association, San Francisco, August 1977.

Frankena, W. *Ethics.* Englewood Cliffs, N.J.: Prentice-Hall, 1963.

Grinder, R. "Parental Child-Rearing Practices, Conscience, and Resistance to Temptation of Sixth-Grade Children. *Child Development,* 1962, *33,* 803-820.

Hoffman, M. "Moral Internalization." In L. Berkowitz (Ed.), *Advances in Experimental Social Psychology,* Vol. 10. New York: Academic Press, 1977.

Hogan, R. "Moral Conduct and Moral Character: A Psychological Perspective." *Psychology Bulletin,* 1973, *79,* 217-232.

Inhelder, B., and Piaget, J. *The Growth of Logical Thinking from Childhood to Adolescence.* New York: Basic Books, 1958.

Keasey, C. B. "Cognitive Implications of Moral Reasonings." In D. DePalma and J. Foley (Eds.), *Moral Development.* Hillsdale, N.J.: L. Erlbaum, 1975.

Kohlberg, L. "The Study of Moral Development." In T. Likona (Ed)., *Moral Development and Behavior.* New York: Holt, Rinehart and Winston, 1976.

Kohlberg, L. "Stage and Sequence: The Cognitive-Developmental Approach to Socialization." In D. A. Goslin (Ed.), *Handbook of Socialization Theory and Research.* Chicago: Rand McNally, 1969.

Kuhn, D., and others. "The Development of Formal Operations in Logical and Moral Judgments." *Genetic Psychology Monographs,* 1977, *95,* 97-188.

Kurtines, W., and Greif, E. "The Development of Moral Thought: Review and Evaluation of Kohlberg's Approach." *Psychological Bulletin,* 1974, *81,* 453-470.

Langer, J. *Theories of Development.* New York: Holt, Rinehart and Winston, 1969.

Nucci, L., and Turiel, E. "Social Interactions and the Development of Social Concepts in Pre-School Children." *Child Development*, 1978, *49*, 400-408.

Nucci, L. "Social Development: Personal, Conventional and Moral Concepts." Unpublished doctoral dissertation, University of California, Santa Cruz, 1977.

Parke, R. D. "Nurturance, Nurturance Withdrawal and Resistance to Deviation." *Child Development*, 1967, *38*, 1101-1110.

Parke, R., and Walters, R. "Some Factors Influencing the Efficacy of Punishment Training for Inducing Response Inhibition." *Monograph of the Society for Research in Child Development*, 1967, *32*, 1-45.

Piaget, J. "Piaget's Theory." In P. H. Mussen (Ed.), *Carmichael's Manual of Child Psychology*. Vol. 1. New York: Wiley, 1970.

Piaget, J. *The Psychology of Intelligence*. Totowa, N.J.: Littlefield, Adams and Company, 1966.

Piaget, J. *Judgment and Reasoning in the Child*. New York: Littlefield, Adams, 1928.

Rawls, J. *A Theory of Justice*. Cambridge, Mass.: Harvard University Press, 1971.

Sears, R. R., and Parke, R. D. "Effect on Resistance to Deviation of Observing a Model's Affective Reactions to Response Consequences." *Developmental Psychology*, 1971, *5*, 40-47.

Sears, R. R., Rau, L., and Alpert, R. *Identification and Child Rearing*. Stanford, Calif.: Stanford University Press, 1965.

Selman, R. "Toward a Structural Analysis of Developing Interpersonal Relations Concepts: Research with Normal and Disturbed Preadolescent Boys." In A. Pick (Ed.), *X Annual Minnesota Symposium on Child Psychology*. Minneapolis: University of Minnesota Press, 1976.

Slaby, R. E., and Parke, R. D. "Effect on Resistance to Deviation of Observing a Model's Reactive Reactions to Response Consequences." *Developmental Psychology*, 1971, *5*, 40-47.

Tomlinson-Keasey, C., and Keasey, C. B. "The Mediating Role of Cognitive Development in Moral Development." *Child Development*, 1974, *45*, 291-298.

Turiel, E. "Social Convention and Morality: Two Distinct Conceptual and Developmental Systems." In C. B. Keasey (Ed.), *Nebraska Symposium on Motivation*. Vol. 25. Lincoln: University of Nebraska Press, forthcoming.

Turiel, E. "The Development of Concepts of Social Structure." In J. Glick and A. Clarke-Stewart (Eds.), *Studies in Social and Cognitive Development*. Vol. 1. New York: Gardner Press, 1978.

Turiel, E. "The Development of Social Concepts: Mores, Customs and Conventions." In D. J. DePalma and F. M. Foley (Eds.), *Moral Development: Current Theory and Research*. Hillsdale, N.J.: L. Erlbaum, 1975.

Turiel, E. "Developmental Processes in the Child's Moral Thinking." In P. Mussen, J. Langer, and M. Covington (Eds.), *Trends and Issues in Developmental Psychology*. New York: Holt, Rinehart and Winston, 1969.

Walters, R., Parke, R., and Cane, V. "Timing of Punishment and the Observation of Consequences to Others as Determinants of Response Inhibition." *Journal of Experimental Child Psychology*, 1965, *2*, 10-30.

Werner, H. "The Concept of Development from a Comparative and Organismic View." In D. Harris (Ed.), *The Concept of Development*. Minneapolis: University of Minnesota Press, 1957.

*Elliot Turiel is a professor of psychology at the University of California, Santa Cruz and a research psychologist at the Institute of Human Development at the University of California, Berkeley.*

*Children's development of a "natural philosophy"*
*is a fundamental part of their social-cognitive growth*
*and influences their real-life relations with the*
*social world as well.*

# development of concepts of self, mind, reality, and knowledge

## john broughton

"Childhood is sensual, materialistic, very dualistic; youth, ideal, optimistic; manhood, realistic, positivistic; and pessimism and especially epistemology are essentially the fit philosophy of old-age if of any period of life."
(Hall, 1904, vol. 2, p. 50)

It is a sign of some progress in the field of "social cognition" that the label itself is coming into serious question. Recent reviews of theory and research have expressed various kinds of uneasiness with the term (Blasi and Hoeffel, 1975; Broughton, 1975, forthcoming (b); Broughton and Riegel, 1977; Chandler, 1974; Shantz, 1975; Sigel, 1975). Some

Thanks are due to Lawrence Kohlberg, James Fowler, Lisa Cross, and Laura Rogers for help with the research reported here. Invaluable advice has also been given in the past by Klaus Riegel, Augusto Blasi, Jane Loevinger, Robert Selman, Edmund Sullivan, Carolyn Shantz, Hans Furth, and Howard Gruber. The subjects of the study deserve my enduring gratitude for their interest, patience, and criticism.

criticisms have been at a general level, for example, the argument that *all* cognition is social since all aspects of thought presuppose an interpersonal constructive process. Others have focused on more specific problems, such as the fact that the traditional interpretation of *social* as meaning interpersonal excludes important areas of self and self-concept on the one hand and institutions and ideology on the other.

The situation is further complicated by a tendency to contrast social cognition and "physical" (or logical) cognition. While these two domains are intuitively different, the criteria that first come to mind for describing the social world turn out to be unconvincing. For example, the social is not more complex; in many ways physical things are more complex, since they are less like us. The social is not less observable or predictable; social science is built on observation and has its laws and universals just like physical science. Recent writers, such as Harre and Secord (1972) have tried to characterize the social as essentially comprising "rule-guided behavior." But the latter criterion is also inadequate since rule-guidedness exists at many levels, some of them physical (Toulmin, 1974), while much social life has nothing to do with rules (Merleau-Ponty, 1963).

The whole notion of physical versus social as a dualism or a polarity breaks down under close inspection. First, insofar as *social* implicates people, it includes physical bodies; insofar as it refers to society, it includes extrapersonal physical structures. Physical and social are therefore not opposites. Second, ontologically speaking, there are types of existence that fall under neither heading. The self, for example, is not physical and is not exhausted by the social. Also, the mental, while related to both physical and social, is reducible to neither. The biological would be another exception. At the level of society, there are such entities as institutions, ideology, and culture that involve, in addition to the physical and social, selves, minds, and biologies—in fact, the whole realm of human action. Third, the physical and social *interpenetrate*, so that what appear to be the most physical aspects of life are often the most social (sex, for example), and what appear to be the most peculiarly social may be quintessentially physical (for example, mechanical-industrial production). Interpenetration means that the one turns into the other, as is apparent in the flux of alienation and dealienation in either sex or industrial production.

Even at the level of scientific methods, the physical and social sciences have no less complicated a relationship. The various methods of science do not fall neatly into one category or the other. Where methods are ascribed to one domain, they are not easily prevented from appropriate application in the other, and most subject matters require an uneasy alliance of both (compare Adorno and others, 1976).

The dichotomy of physical versus social reflects not an objective reality but a particular tradition, both philosophical and ideological, which assumes a "natural" opposition of mind and matter, or of society and physical nature. This perspective aims to simplify things by reducing them to two great categories, so that one can then be explained in terms of the other. Thus, within the Piagetian tradition, all cognition is to be constructed from the basis in the logical-mathematical structures of the physical world. Research then proceeds to show how social cognition is an elaboration of physical cognition. Inductive/deductive inference is still the tool, and cause/effect relations are still the proper object of knowledge. The only difference is that social cognition involves inference about unobservable internal causes of behavior. The ideological commitment to this endeavor in developmental psychology is witnessed by our continued obliviousness to the alternative sociological position, that logical categories and technical reason are derived by abstraction from universal properties of personal and societal life, which are neither unobservable nor inferential.

Part of the Piagetian program is to argue that central to the personality by the time of adolescence is the reflective ego, formed through interaction with the physical world. In finally differentiating itself from the world, the self becomes self-conscious. It does this by virtue of the superimposition of the formal propositional calculus upon the concrete logic of classes and relations, creating a structure of structures that Inhelder and Piaget (1958) claim is tantamount to thinking about thinking. In this way Piagetian theory appears to redeem its promise to explain not just the genesis of logic, but the genesis of epistemology. However, the formal recursion of logic upon itself cannot be equated with thinking about thinking. Logic is not thinking, and formal operations do not think about concrete operations. Anyway, "thinking about thinking" is a poor way to characterize reflection. Reflection implies consciousness, which includes much more than thought, and it implies self-consciousness (Lonergan, 1967), an awareness of self as subject that cannot be accounted for by formal logic (Blasi and Hoeffel, 1974; Broughton, 1977a). Furthermore, reflection cannot be equated with an epistemology, which is more precisely a theory of knowledge.

The possibility therefore arises that there remains to be defined empirically a cognitive developmental epistemology that is something other than a derivative of Piagetian formal intelligence and that continues to develop after early adolescence. This is foreshadowed speculatively in Hegel's philosophical-historical stages of self-consciousness, interpreted more specifically in terms of psychological stages in the theoretical work of James Mark Baldwin, the originator of genetic epistemology (Baldwin, 1906-1911; Broughton and Freeman-Moir, forthcoming). For Baldwin, the appropriate epistemic domain was a comprehensive one of "genetic logic," comprising a "functional logic" (theory of knowledge) and a "real logic" (theory of reality).

Following a similar path, the study to be reported here explores qualitative cognitive levels in the child's progressive differentiation and integration of a "natural philosophy," which we might think of as the individual's naive epistemology and metaphysics. The subject matter of research was how thinking about knower and known, self and reality, develops. The aim was to provide a preliminary developmental scheme for the description of psychological frameworks linking concepts of self, mind, reality, and knowledge.

From Baldwin's theory and some pilot data, an extensive semi-structured questionnaire was developed. The questions required subjects to demonstrate, define, and reflect on their intuitive understanding of a variety of epistemological and metaphysical relationships: self/world, mental/material, person/thing, physical/social, reality/appearance, knower/known, subjective/objective, absolute/relative, fact/theory, truth/falsehood, and thought/feeling. Subjects' responses were probed with further inquiries in order to identify the grounds for their judgments and to clarify ambiguous statements. This is essentially the method of "critical exploration" (Piaget, 1929, pp. 1-31).

Interviewees were thirty-six male and female subjects, ages ten, fourteen, eighteen, twenty-two, and twenty-six, residing in middle class suburban Boston, and of mixed ethnicity and religion. Up to age eighteen, the subjects were typical students of slightly above-average intelligence. The twenty-two- and twenty-six-year-olds were, respectively, undergraduates and postgraduates selected from a wide range of disciplines. In the interest of scope and clarity, other interviews will be referred to in this chapter that were supplementary to the main study, especially in regard to the younger age bracket, which has only been informally sampled as yet.

From transcripts of the interviews, an initial set of levels or "ideal types" were drawn up (Table 1). This was done through a complex procedure of interpretation, cross-comparison, and abstraction, which aimed at identifying the grounds most generally given by subjects for their judgments. The flavor of these age-related frameworks can be partly illustrated by the following, given in response to the question "What is the self?"

Six-year-old: *It's a body.*

Ten-year-old: *Your self is you.*

Fourteen-year-old: *The mental self is just the way you think, the physical self is sort of the way you are biologically.*

Eighteen-year-old: *A separate unit individual.*

Twenty-two-year-old: *It's a philosophical invention . . . somebody made up to sell deodorant.*

Twenty-six-year-old: *Some mechanism that processes the interaction between what I am at the moment, and what is going on outside me.*

Even in these examples it is possible to see three phases: a predualistic childhood period, followed in adolescence by the emergence of the "great dualisms" (such as mental/physical), which in adulthood the individual attempts to reconcile through a truly reflective awareness of self, reality, and knowledge. Two levels within each of these major phases will now be described in detail.

### level 1 (approximate age range 4–7)

Baldwin compared the initial psychological levels to the orientation of the pre-Socratic Greeks. Theirs was primarily an ontological frame of reference, in which reality had an absolute, external quality. In the child, this is manifest in a crude kind of naive realism. There is no distinction between subject and object. Self and reality are simply *presumed.* They are existing, external, and self-evident physical things, which are sensed directly. Knowledge is automatic. Truth is one, absolute, and known by authority. The interview questions, while generally not incomprehensible, are viewed with wonder or suspicion, the child not understanding how or why such questions could be asked about a patent here-and-now reality, particularly by an adult. There is a failure to realize any problematic aspect to realness as witnessed by this interchange with five-year-old Alan:

(How do you know that chest is really over there?) *They put it there.* (How do you know that house is over there?) *That's where they built it.*

**Table 1. Levels of Natural Philosophy by Category**

| Level | Self/World | Mental/Material | Physical/Social | Reality/Appearance | Knower/Known |
|---|---|---|---|---|---|
| 1. Objective (age 4–7) | Presumptive: Self-evident, bodily self. Not differentiated from reflexive "itself." | Adualist: Gross head/body distinction. Visible and invisible not differentiated. Mind and body mutually permeable. | Animistic: Living and nonliving only partly distinguished. People distinguished from things only along quantitative physical dimensions. | Objective: Reality presumed. Simple and immediate existence of external things. Real undifferentiated from nonartificial. | Dogmatic: Thought and its objects undifferentiated. Direct, automatic knowing. Single extrinsic truth, known and handed down by authority. |
| 2. Individual (age 8–12) | Individual: Self is specific person, me or you. Perceiving, acting person. Source or agent. | Organic: Mind differentiated from body as brainlike organ controlling rest of body. Discrete, nonvisible mental contents. | Subjective: People distinguished as conscious, sentient, or as self-active individuals. Body is (subordinate) part of person. | Native realist: Certainty of reality directly sensed. Appearance is the way something "looks" and this is reality. Real differentiated from imaginary as persistent. | Empirical: Partial differentiation of knower from known. Experience directly caused by object. Subjective not opposed to objective. Truth is absolute fact, is opposed to lie, and is individually apprehended and asserted. |
| 3. Divided (age 12+) | Divided: Self is mind (mental self) more than body (physical self). Unique subjective traits, opinions, beliefs, or values. Authentic inner self differentiated from false outer appearance (social personality or role self). | Immature dualist: Abstract mental differentiated from concrete physical as a fluid and invisible medium. Mental and physical as shared classes with interdependence (overlap). | Interpersonal: People have personality and show themselves to other people. Body is appearance, ambiguous. Physical as impersonal "scientific" world. | Realist: Appearance generally realistic, but mind may add personal distortion (opinion or value). Mental is belief rather than reality. | Social: Concrete facts known by individuals. Truth as interpersonal demonstration and plausibility (overlap). Nascent skepticism. |
| 4. Dualist (age 18+) | Substantial: Self as system: soul, intellect, logic, identity, or "cogito" (self-control). Self has mental and physical attributes. Self-concept, or "me," rather than "I." Generalized self or perspective. | Cartesian: Dualism between objective mechanistic system of scientific cause/effect, and subjective or spiritual world of belief, purpose, and reason. Unconscious differentiated from conscious. | Individual: Social as system of abstract individuals. People as spiritual, self-regulating, and purposeful (vitalist). instances of the general rule. Body now estranged as part of material world (mechanist). | Dualist: Reality assumed. Noumenon differentiated from phenomenon. Substantial reality is lawlike system generating appearances (data). | Positivist: Knowledge is inductive generalization of observation, constructive copy of world. Truth, which subordinates reality, is replicable and is achieved through social-conventional testing of models. Impartial "generalized other" defines objective standpoint. |

| | | | | | |
|---|---|---|---|---|---|
| 5. *Subjective* (age 20+) | *Process:* Self as flux of experience, or process of self-realization. Breakdown of substantial soul or identity. Everything has self. | *Reductionist:* Monistic materialism. Mind as epiphenomenon. | *Anarchist:* Fusion of natural and social. (Either reduction of social to biological or panpsychism.) Dialectic of organization and anarchic chaos. | *Subjectivist:* All reality phenomenal. Full determinism at level of data. | *Relativist:* All knowledge is subjective, or arbitrary convention. Opposition to objectification. Skepticism and solipsism. |
| 6. *Rational* (age 25+) | *Epistemological:* Self as transcendental ego, or function of universal self-consciousness. Self-conceiver or subject-self differentiated from empirical or object-self. | *Parallelist:* Functional "mental" and "physical," psychology versus physiology, as ideational systems of explanatory constructs. | *Rational:* Social as rational democratic organization, versus natural as nonrational but systematic sphere. Natural law. Physical and social sciences. | *Perspectivist:* Reality presupposed. Reality defined by coherence and utility of system within which it is interpreted. | *Methodological:* Objective relativism. Knowledge and truth defined by intersubjective use of paradigm, such as idealism, behaviorism, etc. Logical level distinguished from empirical. |
| 7. *Dialectical Materialist* | *Historical:* Self as trans-individual subject (e.g., class subject), transforming natural/social reality. | *Interpenetrative:* Dialectical materialism. Nature and culture penetrate each other through human activity (work). | *Dialectical:* Natural world transformed into cultural, or alienated from it through domination. | *Materialist:* Objective material reality dynamically evolving and appearing through human activity. | *Social:* Knowledge as active, social transformation of reality through man-made, historical categories. |

The reality of all things is obvious and is not yet differentiated from their appearance. Thoughts are real because they are not differentiated from their objects. The "real" is typically contrasted with the "fake," meaning artificial or man-made, and not with the unreal or nonexistent.

Knowledge is having the correct or proper response. Seven-year-old Laura says, *Like there are a lot of answers to things in your head. . . . Every single answer is in your brain, that you should know.* Being told these answers is combined with direct experience as a source of knowledge, as we can see from six-year-old Lenny:

> (How can you come to know about something?) *If you, if someone told you, and they know. If they're sure.* (How do they come to know?) *Someone else told them.* (Oh. And it goes back and back and back?) *Yeah.* (Who told the first person?) *They just looked.*

Note that there is no mediation of knowledge, since nothing is lost or gained in the telling.

The person, too, has an obvious physical quality. It is a bodily self, where self just means "itself" (so that dead people and even objects have a self). Of course, the terms *physical* and *bodily* here must not be taken literally, since there is no notion of the physical proper, as yet. There is no distinction between mind and body, a state of affairs that Baldwin called *adualism.* The term *mind* is not used spontaneously but is assimilated under "brain." This in turn tends to be grossly identified with the head, the anatomical source of bodily movement. As a result, there are scant grounds for distinguishing people from animals, or even living things from nonliving things, except on the basis of contingent quantitative differences (they are larger, softer, and so on). Another exchange with five-year-old Alan shows some of these level 1 characteristics:

> (What is your mind?) *The mind is your head, isn't it?* (What does it do? What's it for?) *I don't know . . . because I don't know what minds are.* (Do people have minds?) *Yes.* (Anything besides people have minds?) *No.* (Your dog?) *He has a mind.* (How do you know? *Everything that moves. Or walks.*

*Five-year-old Sally expresses a similar notion:*

(Do trees have minds?) *Yeah. They can move.* (How?) *When they saw it down.*

Weakly defined and poorly delimited, mental and physical show little differentiation, either in terms of spatial segregation or visibility/invisibility. For six-year-old Ian, the mind goes through the body and it helps other things.

(How does it do that?) *It flows through the body like two ghosts flying.* (Can your thoughts be in your body?) *Yes. The blood takes them.*

### level 2 (approximate age range 8-12)

The second childhood level, still predualistic, does exhibit a partial differentiation of the subjective from the objective. A purely naive realism is relinquished, although the empirical orientation is maintained. *Esse est percipi* ("to be is to be seen") is a good epithet for level 2 thinkers, for whom the idea of a perceiving organism succeeds the earlier notion of immediate presence. While reality is constant and absolute, it undergoes a partial sensory mediation in its passage from outer to inner. For example, ten-year-old Elizabeth talks of a sense of reality, *You'd know if you were imagining a table. You just feel that it isn't there. You'd have some imaginary sense that you're feeling it. A sort of tingly feeling inside tells you that you're really touching it or not really touching it.* This cognitive change reflects Piaget's (1929) observation that concepts of sense emerge during the later phase of childhood. A very precocious, level 2 six-year-old, when asked how he knew there was a real world, replied:

*Because the houses look real.* (What makes them look real?) *They are real. They feel real. I feel them. It feels kind of cementy and woodish.*

There is now an objective, enduring quality to real materials. They look real because they are real, and they are real because they feel real, to *me*. The real is now spontaneously contrasted with the nonexistent. Imagination is understood to exist, as Elizabeth shows above, but it does not usually interfere, because *you know when you're imagining,* and *he can't feel me unless he imagines really hard* (said by

Kevin, also ten). *I couldn't be imagining it [the world] because I wouldn't be imagining for nine years.* In fact, *You can't imagine something that isn't there,* says the same boy. Things are not generally conceived as appearing different from what they are. You just see "what is there" (what is persistent), and what is there naturally has a real look, because (as our six-year-old pointed out) it *is* real. Things look different from reality because of "mistakes," or "if you're farsighted," but these are not major problems, because they do not persist.

Truth has a parallel status. It is known by "going and looking for yourself," "finding out yourself." Another may mediate reality but can mediate it falsely only by lying. You know what the other says is true because he "doesn't laugh" or is "willing to bet on it." Facts can likewise imply matters of individual assertion. For example, when asked what a fact is, ten-year-old George replies, *If I say 'try hamburgers,' and you say 'they're good,' then that's a fact.* While knowledge and truth are connected with individuals, the question of differences in what people hold to be true or real was not raised spontaneously by any of the ten-year-old subjects. Where the possibility of conflicting interpretations is explicitly raised by the interviewer, truth (that is, reality) is simply affirmed with an absolute individual objectivity, as in the case of Kevin:

> We know who's right. . . . You just do. Our brain tells us (Which person do we believe?) Me. (Why?) Because that's the way it is.

This limitation shows to what extent the subjective still has a primitive articulation at level 2 of reflective thought. In addition, the limited quality of the nascent subjective is equally visible in the level 2 concepts of mind and body. While there is not yet a division of reality into mental and physical, the word *mind* starts to be used spontaneously for a part of the head that is distinguished as a brainlike organ. It is "a lot smarter than the other parts of your body," according to ten-year-old Clem. There appear to be two alternative ways to "organify" mind: either by positing it as a separate organ with an integrity of its own (as does Elisabeth below) or by denying the distinction and identifying it with the brain (as does Julia):

> Elisabeth (ten years): *Mind and brain are like together in the same place. They like work together.* (Could a brain surgeon see the brain?) *He could see the brain. Not the mind I don't think. I don't know. Like I guess you could see the mind.* (What

would it look like?) *Oh, messed up and curled together with the brain.* (The mind is harder to see?) *Yeah, because the brain's bigger.* (How small is the mind?) *It's got to be small enough to fit in your head, so it would probably be three or four inches.*

Julia (ten years): (What is the mind?) *The brain.* (The same thing?) *Yeah.* (Is it different from the brain at all?) *I don't think so.* (Why are there two words then?) *So people can use two different words. So if they don't understand the other word, they can talk about the other word.*

Even (paradoxically) in individuals who equate mind with brain, there is some initial differentiation of function. While mind and brain share thinking and deciding, there is a tendency to see mind as imagining and dreaming, and the brain as having a more executive function (Broughton, forthcoming (a)). With respect to the body, the mind or brain controls the initiation and restriction of activity in a simple master/slave relationship. George states, *But your brain just tells you to. Just like Pinocchio and Jiminy Cricket. . . . Like if the mind didn't control the self, you would jump right out the window any day. . . . The mind controls you, tells you not to jump out the window.*

At level 2, there also arises a primitive notion of mental contents (thoughts, images) distinct from their referential objects as well as from their container. These contents are restricted to the mind or brain and cannot "flow through the body." They are invisible things — discrete and not yet seen in terms of process. They are nonvisible, "not solid" rather than immaterial. This does not prevent them from being real. Asked about the reality of thought, for example, George echoes the sentiment mentioned above with respect to imagination:

(But is that thought real?) *Yes, you're really thinking about it. Because you can sort of hear yourself think it. You can't be thinking and not know, like. You can't really hear yourself. You just know.*

The initial, partial differentiations of mind from body and of thought from thing help both in the child's discrimination of persons from objects and in the child's specification of a self. The latter is inchoate, to a degree commensurate with the limited subjectivity so far noted. The self is an individual source or agent. When asked what changes about himself, Kevin responds:

*My attitudes towards people, and towards the way I think. (Is that part of you?) Yeah, because the way I do and what I do is part of me because it's me doing it.*

When asked what the self is, he replies as follows, revealing how close "self" is to "person." *The person who is saying it. It means him and it doesn't mean anybody else.* The self or person is closely related to his name, as Clem reveals:

(What about yourself, what is it?) *My self is Clem, a person who was born on the planet Earth.*

However, he continues, showing how this individual achieves a degree of free will, self-awareness, and subjective uniqueness:

*I am one of a kind. (What does that mean?) There could be a person who looks like me or talks like me, but no one who has every single detail I have. Never a person who thinks exactly like me. (Why not?) Because when one person talks, the other would talk at the same time, and they'd never be able to exchange sentences.*

Self-consciousness per se is not yet articulated reflectively, even though these ten-year-olds may have reached the level of formal operational thought. It is confined to a sense of "me," the way I look or sound (as with Clem above) or of what I think and what I do (as with Kevin). These are qualities with persistence but not yet conceptualized as traits. Personality is not differentiated from self, and both are close in meaning to "person": *A personality, it's really sort of what you are. . . . A personality's sort of inside you, and you know that you're a certain person.*

### level 3 (from twelve onwards)*

In early adolescence, a third level of consciousness emerges, one which makes the first reflective distinction between mental and physical realities, and between reality and appearance. These divisions pervade ideas about the self, which along with knowledge displays both subjective and objective aspects. Truth is brought into question for the first time.

*Except where otherwise indicated, the examples in this section are from fourteen-year-olds.

Level 2 construed the mind/body problem as simply that—a relation between individual minds and bodies. Level 3 interprets the issue as one of mental and physical, which are qualities shared by individuals. They are, however, not yet substances so much as *classes* of things, spontaneously used to explain the makeup of persons.

> Colin: (What is the self?) *I think it means not just the person, but the inside of the person. Each person is the self, different from another person. Because each person is different in the way their mind works.* (Can you tell me how a person's mind works?) *It is not physical. It is an emotional or mental thing like that.*

> Jack: *Your mind is what you do in your brain. Like your mind, you think. The brain is the matter itself. The mind is more the energy thing. You can't see energy, but you can see matter. Energy is in matter, but matter isn't in energy.* (How is the energy in the matter?) *The energy is what makes it work, right? Gasoline makes a car engine work.* (But gasoline is matter.) *Right. But put the two matters together creates energy.*

It is interesting to note how mind is still conceptualized as a kind of fluid of rarefied matter. Some refer to it as electricity.

Mental and physical are not yet mutually exclusive substances at level 3. There is, in fact, great difficulty in differentiating the two. The overlap is thought of as a kind of personified dependence, says Carrie, [*The mind*] *has a responsibility. It has to—without the mind there wouldn't be anything here. . . . It stays as long as it's supposed to.* While mind overlaps with body, it is no longer seen as a body part or organ. It *is* the brain, but in a new and more differentiated sense. Carrie, for example, says the mind is "the whole brain," meaning that it is an invisible faculty, presence, or activity. *The mind is what goes on in the brain,* says Art.

Along with the description of mind as activity comes a stress on its volitional and intentional qualities. *It is everything you do. And like voluntary control of the body, the mind controls everything the body does.* While the notion of unidirectional control is continued from childhood, the mind is not just the brain. It involves a component of will and valuation. *With our minds we can make our own judgments, and do what we feel is right,* and *It [the mind] decides between alternative ways of doing it, on the basis of their consequences.* Mind is conscious ideas, feelings, and opinions, pragmatically deciding the right and wrong things to do.

As will, the mental is variable. It "isn't the instinctive things," to quote Carrie. In contrast, the physical is involuntary, automatic, and standardized. Sara, asked what the self is, shows (like Colin above) how this notion makes the physical self less central: *The inner side, the mind mostly. How the mind works. Because your body is your outside, but yourself is more your mind. . . . It's just your mind—the way your thoughts go. There are physical things that everybody has, and they are still a part of you, but a more minor part.* The self is a unique mental trait, disposition, or style—"the way your thoughts go"—a possibility created by the emergence of invisible mental *processes*. But it is not sufficient that the mind stands apart from the uniform physical self. It must also stand out from standardized crowd mentality. Otherwise the self turns into a not-self—an alienated copy or fake.

> Meg: (What is the self?) *Being yourself, acting natural . . . not phony. . . . The self is something you want people to see. It's natural in one way and phony in another. I mean I think everybody is really phony, but you're trying to act natural. The mind . . . is what you really think inside you . . . and sometimes you're scared to say. And the self is something you kind of like imitate.*

While the content of self is mental traits, its metaphysical form is ambiguous. In line with the dualizing at this level, there emerges Laing's "divided self"—a split between the real inner self and the social appearance or personality through which self is made manifest to others (Broughton, forthcoming (a)). Perhaps this underlies and explains an interesting phenomenon of adolescence referred to by Erikson (1968, p. 135): "A sometimes precocious self-transcendence seems to be felt strongly in a transient manner in youth, as if a pure identity had to be kept free from psycho-social encroachment."

"I" and "me," self-in-itself and self-for-others, are put into tension with each other for the first time. Self-consciousness, however, is protected from inauthenticity, being confined within the "I." There is immediate and complete self-knowledge, and no unconscious. The "me" part, conversely, implies an interpersonal self rather than a strictly individual one, which vitiates the possibility of truly knowing the other. Jack says: *I know exactly what I want, and how I like it, and I know what I feel about things. And I don't know someone else.*

A parallel doubt is introduced into the apprehension of the rest of the world. Because of the subjectivity of the mind, others can question your perception. *They could say 'Your mind is messed up.'* 'Your mind is tricking you,' says Carrie, who goes on to explain that this is why *you have to—you need an opinion. You need the support of someone saying 'That's good.'* Thus, like the outer self, truth becomes interpersonal. However, it resides ultimately in a feeling of interpersonal comfort that is not "objective" in the usual sense of the word. Truth is a matter of acceptance and plausibility. Truth comes *from people wanting it to be truth all the time,* as Rob said. Knower and known merge in a fashion similar to the overlapping of mental and physical, or one individual and another.

### level four (from eighteen onwards)

In the late adolescence or early adulthood of some individuals, there emerges a dualism consisting of two completely separate and mutually exclusive systems or categories of substance. The physical world now gains an internal structure and a certain degree of autonomy by virtue of being regulated by a fixed scientific order of mechanical cause and effect. Vera, a twenty-six-year-old, says, *I believe in action/reaction. Something happens, something caused it. And that is a whole world view.*

Level 4 attempts to find a systematic connection or correspondence between the two halves of reality—mental and physical—but this is made difficult by their mutually exclusive relationship. The mental moiety remains a source of puzzlement.

> Vera: *There is something that goes on in your mind that is real, at the basic level of electron flows. . . . It is measurable, and it is a reaction, a thing. . . . Now I don't know how to trace from an electron flow to an idea in my mind. . . . It is a reaction to that electron flow, and therefore it is real. It is a belief. I believe it but I can't prove it. . . . Maybe the mind is part of the brain we don't understand.*

The idea of thoughts is more romantic 'than just chemicals,' echoes Mary, age twenty-two. Because knowledge is reluctantly defined as a scientific kind of understanding, mind still has a mysterious or religious quality—the realm of the unknown. However, unlike level 3, level 4 does construe the mental as qualitatively different—as a reality in itself, requiring a separate kind of explanation.

> Wade (twenty-two years): *From my point of view, the brain is the physical machine that makes the mind go. If you believe in*

*life after death, if you believe in a soul, then the brain is kind of like a physical explanation to satisfy people about the definition of the mind. And the mind is something above that. I don't know if I believe that. . . . No one quite understands how it works. I don't think we'll ever find out.. . . . It's something to do with the electric charges in the brain. It's incomprehensible to me that electric charges could do that, but it seems more logical than the mind just being because God made it so. . . . There are just such opposite things: electrons on the one side, and mental images on the other. No one knows how they're joined. There are scientific explanations for it, mechanical explanations. They can tell you how it happens but not why.* (What would be why?) *I can't explain why I see the lamp here. That lamp, the light rays hit my eye. That's the explanation, but—I'm talking about the transfer of physical properties to the mental properties. . . . You don't actually see the lamp, you see the image or the thought of the lamp . . . what it's called.*

The strict dualism here leads to epistemological consequences, to a "copy theory of knowledge," with a segregation of noumenon and phenomenon and no way to relate them. *The chair should exist independently of people seeing it. . . . If I go out of the room, that chair's still 'appearing' to be there, even though I would never see it.* This is Wade's reference to the noumenon. On the other hand, he knows that *it is all a person's perception. That chair is a chair. If it appeared different to someone else, then it would be a distortion in his perception. Most people would see it as a chair.* At the end here we see his solution. Since "it is all a person's perception," the only possible definition of truth is by convention. He keeps referring to "this definition of the real world," and says, *"Things exist because people perceive them to exist, and they're given the definitions . . . I guess a majority of people agree on definitions, and that's how a definition is.* Vera takes a very similar position to Wade's, illustrating how truth may eventually come to subordinate reality: *You always see the appearance of something . . . Appearance means things. It appears differently to you than it might appear to someone else . . . the reality being by more democratic vote. . . . They are all going to say that their seeing reality is the only measure we have, is by consensus. . . . If you are taking a vote, you are voting on what appearance is the most correct representation of reality. You are guessing which reality is real."*

Although each individual perceives a true aspect, and as Wade says, *What you think is the most important, as far as you're concerned,* Wade's collectivist approach to truth works because there is something more at stake: *Everyone perceives things through different filters. You need to integrate all the filters. . . . Take all the different points, and find some picture of the whole. . . . Because you see more and more aspects of a different thing. But then you're talking about a human reality if you integrate over all people.* Reality is a wanted criminal for whom the police have no mug shot. The objective mind is a "pattern recognizer" that, like a police artist, forms a composite picture by superimposing the partial identifications of different witnesses. Note that this makes knowledge exclusively experiential and essentially sensory. To sustain the notion of mind as model maker, it must be created in the image of the material world. It must be seen as filtering out and encoding the recurrent regularities in experience by some process of mechanistic association and data reduction. The known—the recurrent pattern—becomes a general image, stereotype, or definition. The knower is the generalized other who takes an impartial, objective perspective.

Much as there is a substantial lawful reality independent of its knowers at level 4, there is a substantial self, too. As we have seen, on epistemological grounds, our level 4 interviewees already resisted the elimination of their personal, intellectual, romantic aspect that is beyond the senses. One level 4 subject says, for example, *You can know every aspect of the chemical. Whereas to me you just can't know every aspect of a person.* What is this additional quality? Even though the mental is seen as differentiated from the physical by being outside law, it has to be defined in terms of its own internal regulation, its formal, systematic quality. When asked what is part of the self, Vera says, *Type of thinking is, probably. The way a person uses or doesn't use logic. A type of planning. A way of running your life or not running it.*

Similarly, for Bob (age twenty-two):

> *[The self is] the way your mind puts things in a logical progression—thought patterns. . . . I think the self is the life force in a logical progression.* (Is that the same thing?) *Well, no. Life force is the thing that motivates you, but the logical progression is just the intellect, the thought processes of the self.*

For Bob, this inner self is quite separate from his corporeal self: *I mean, the body for me is just an appearance, is just a shadow. It's the living force inside you; you know, the ideas that emanate, that are the self.* In this sense, the self is soul, the noumenal essence or being of someone. Jim (eighteen years) replies as follows when asked what the self is: *I don't know. The self, you can describe it as the soul of one, the inner thing that makes him go . . . giving you a reason for being. The soul is completely separate. It is so much higher up.* The notion of soul is a two-edged sword. It individuates, but it is also something we all have in common. Our high school senior, Jim, says of the body: *In some people it differs. But I also say it links you to the rest of them. It gives you an identity with man.* But he sees a problem here. *Because you are a part of mankind, your thoughts are always related to someone else's thoughts.* There is potential here for absorption into some reified "group mind." As a result, *There has to be a part that takes it apart from that huge mass . . . [so] that there is still a self,* says Mary. Hence Jim defines his self as *an individual in that society, a separate unit individual. . . . The soul is the essence of identity in the self.*

This seems to be what Harre and Secord (1972) are talking about when they define persons by their "self-direction," or as "self-monitoring agents" autonomous in spite of external influences. It is a negative self-definition. For Bob, it is the ability to say, in defiance of norms: *I will not. I cannot and I will not.* It is a resistance against some external force trying to invade the self. Resistance to outer control requires an internalized self-control. Self-control is central to consciousness and self. What makes something part of your self for Bob is when you *integrate it into yourself* rather than *allowing yourself to be sold on something. I think you have to convince yourself. You know, sit down and say, 'Well, of course. It's logical. Of course I believe it.'*

Since mind copies matter, and knowledge in general is prediction and control, knowing implies a conformity. Keith, an undergraduate, points this out: *Only when people understand the laws are they able to make their behavior conform with the laws and thereby control those laws.*

Self-control, however, is self-knowledge, which defines the individual, taking it apart from the mass. Self-regulation is a kind of self-conformity that can *bring you alone with yourself* (Mary), much as the logical core of self is *entirely self-contained* (Vera). Complementary to this concept of consciousness, the idea of the unconscious now arises. As Mary says: *There are so many other parts of the way one is, and unconscious things that people do. The self is not always conscious of itself, or of its being, so that you can't have that control.*

Self-control is the faculty of the soul, intellect, or identity that is "so much higher up," making people "spiiritual" beings, "on a different plane," who are "aware of the life force itself.." This self-awareness often brings with it the notion of self as an empirical self-concept. Says Paul: *[The self is] what a person thinks of himself, how he thinks he handles things.* Whereas Wade states that: *The self is what you are, what I think Wade to be. . . . You know how you act in certain situations . . . and you know what to expect of yourself.* This amounts to a generalized self, corresponding to the generalized other implied in the conventional view of knowledge discussed above. The reflection of the "I" on the "me" — the self-concept — is just the observable "me." Reflection is like all knowledge: It is prediction and control of empirical regularities. Such inductive knowledge of the self's patterns is the necessary basis for self-control. As in psychology at large, conceiving the self as self-concept tends to make the "I" vestigial, leaving out the self as self-conceiver (Broughton and Riegel, 1977). It is the task of later levels to recapture this lost subjectivity.

By whatever name this noumenal self-observing force exerting inner control is called, it is given the characteristics usually ascribed by philosophers to substance (Cassirer, 1923; Frondizi, 1953). These are individuation (discreteness and independence), permanence, uniqueness, self-identity, personality, transcendence, and the possession of attributes through which it is manifested and from which it is inferred.

Finally, the permanence and personal identity of sameness of the self as soul is no longer the retaining of specific opinions, values, or character traits, as it was at level 3. It is the system or structural relation of parts to whole. Paul borrows a metaphor from his undergraduate specialty, (geology):

> *The basis of the whole thing stays the same.* (Is it the same self?) *It can be the same self, but in a different form.* (The same material?) *The same composition.*

Thus, in internal structure, self is characterized by the same kind of systematic interrelatedness that typifies mind/body, knowledge, and reality at this level. At level 4, the metaphysical problem underlying all categories is the relation of general to particular, and the two poles of force (or control) and law (logic form) provide the basic concepts through which the parts can be made to cohere into wholes.

### level 5 (from twenty onwards)

At the fifth level, the possibility of a thoroughgoing relativity of knowledge that was latent in the concept of the mysterious and the noumenal at level 4 is brought to fruition. The noumenon or substance becomes completely absorbed in the phenomenon. The discovery is made that nothing is given in itself, that all text has context. A leap of inference is made to the conclusions that impartiality is a pretense and that there can be no objectivity.

In place of substance, sameness, and self and reality as system, subjects in this phase emphasize process, difference, and the subjective, relative, and material. Earlier notions of soul and objective truth are treated as reifications, and an attempt is made to interpret all existence reductionistically in terms of material process. Higher human aspirations tend to be reduced to their common biological basis. In the quest for an abstract individual freedom of self, the conception of knowledge perilously approaches solipsism. Consciousness is relation, relation is all things, and all things are conscious, or have selves. Objects of awareness, previously assumed to be different in nature from the mind aware of them, are now found to have a natural identity with consciousness.

The breakdown of the substantial dualism can be seen in twenty-two-year-old- Kathy's response to the question "What is the mind?":

> The mind is the brain, the actual physical brain. (It's same as the brain?) Yeah. (Any difference between mind and brain?) No. . . . Mind is matter that knows how to do tricky things. It is special kinds of cells or something, special chemicals.

Skepticism about a separate mental substance is extended to a loss of faith in the self as something apart from the process of the body. Asked "What is the self?", Kathy responds: I think it is wrong to say you have a self. You are what you see, what the body can do. . . . So I don't really believe in the self. It's a philosophical invention . . . somebody made up to sell deodorant.

This breakdown of self as substance, which we might see as parallel to Erikson's late adolescent "identity crisis," involves a heightened sense of reflectivity. The self loses independent permanent existence in the flux of relative perceptions in the perception of perceptions, which comes to define what people are, as opposed to other things. Kathy demonstrates this:

> (What makes up a person?) It's a tangled web. A person's nature exists mostly in the minds of the people who he

*interacts with. And a person's concept of his own nature exists mostly in the minds of the people who he interacts with. And a person's concept of his own nature exists in what he thinks others think of him.*

Much as self is reduced to interpersonal perspectives, so is reality. The individual person has become the thinker of his or her own thoughts and hence the thinker of reality. Cognition is active construction of the world. It therefore makes no sense to talk about noumenal things-in-themselves, or selves-in-themselves, or to attach more than an arbitrary significance to conventional truth. As Kathy says: *There could be an unsubjective reality, and that could be what the mind reflects. But that unsubjective reality would just be arbitrary. It would not matter to anyone because no one would be able to see it. So in that sense it would be unreal. . . . It seems kind of academic.*

## level 6

While physical reality was "lawful" at level 4, level 6 elaborates a reflective concept of law that can be applied to the mental realm as well as the physical one. This application establishes social sciences as well as natural sciences as legitimate rational pursuits. Though maintaining the belief that things are only given in relation to one another, the level 6 individual does not leap to a conclusion that there can be no objectivity. Rather it is precisely the job of rational laws to account for the nature of relations.

What this means at level 6 is that people must become epistemologists in their thinking about reality. It no longer suffices to make a radical split between mind and reality as at levels 4 and 5, fudging it first making truth entirely objective (level 4) and then by making it entirely subjective (level 5). The only resolution is to set up criteria distinguishing subjective and objective *within* experience and thus defining what is objective knowing and what is subjective. Another way of saying this is that the subjective world of thought is subdivided into rational and irrational, where the criteria defining rationality are coherence within a categorical system and the sharedness of the paradigm or system. Roy (age twenty-six) says:

*[Truth] isn't observable. You can't get truth directly from observation. That's run through with the categories of your own mind.* (How do you prove something true?) *You prove it true by giving reasons. And the reasons that you give also re-*

*flect your categories.* (What do you mean "run through with the categories of your own mind"?) *You can use the categories that you have to sort the data coming in, to understand, to give meaning to those experiences. . . . That's the process of interpretation. The categories you have aren't purely personal. You gained them through experience of other's writings, and other minds. You adopt some from outside and develop some on your own. You use whatever works.*

Where level 5 rejected self on the grounds that it has no substance, level 6 accepts instead that self is the self-determining function of experience, that which is necessary for and constitutes experience. That is, self is conceived of at level 6, for the first time epistemologically, as *knower.* Self is rational self-awareness, comprising a reflective perspective that critically interprets self and world alike. Instead of being just "me" (self-concept or others' concepts of me), self is also a transcendent "I" the conceiver of self and all other things. Asked "What is the self?" Roy replies:

*Whole ways I see myself. Although I am reacting to objective conditions (the existence of other things and people in the outside world), the perception of it is my own. There's some kind of filtering process that's filtering those and bringing them through to me in terms of my own feelings. Some mechanism that processes the interaction between what I am at the moment, and what is going on outside me. . . . The part of me that sees myself is closer to the core of what myself is.*

Yet there is a certain universality to self as well. *Part of it is seeing that part of the other person's self that is and could be you, yourself,* says Mick (twenty-six). A point that Baldwin makes about the mature notion of subjectivity is that while subjectivity is singularity, it is a *general* or universal property of individuals and does not imply that we are each unique cells walled off from each other. What binds us together at this level of the universal meaning of logical unity is our common function of shared self-awareness, realized as common and as an ideal defining property of humanity. For the first time at this level, a set of explicit logical polarities become of central concern: unity/difference, general/particular, potential/actual, permanence/change, and so on. This is because the notion of knowing as reason—a transformation of reality with an internal logical structure—has been distinguished from empirical fact.

Since we have moved from substance to function in concepts of reality and self, why not in mind and body? What were originally distinct mental and physical substances at level 4 and were reduced to material substrate and epiphenomenon at level 5 are now interpreted as categories within experience, as different functional accounts of the same thing. Natalie (twenty-six) says, *Mental and physical are two different systems of description describing me, or my brain. Each have their own laws.* According to Nick (twenty-six): *We come to find out about this one thing in two different ways. . . . The laws that apply to mental states are not the same laws as apply to brain states.* The fact that the dualism of substances has been replaced by a dualism of methods (compare Toulmin, 1974) is reason to suspect that level 6 presents its own problems, to be resolved perhaps at a further level yet to be defined and observed.

## conclusion

While no higher level than six was exhibited by the subjects interviewed, there are reasons to suspect that a seventh level exists; we have seen that dualism, idealism, and relativism remain. If Hegel, Cassirer, Baldwin, and Piaget are to be believed, the parallels between intellectual history and cognitive development allow us to make reasonable inferences about the latter from our knowledge of the former. Historically, level 6 as described here would represent some form of idealism, perhaps with a pragmatist tinge to it. Historically, such a proposition undergoes further development even within idealism (compare Hegel's and Baldwin's higher stages of self-consciousness) and then undergoes radical criticism and revision at the hands of dialectical materialism. These historical facts must eventually be reflected in a developmental psychology of philosophy, because the materialist dialectic demonstrates and then resolves logical and practical contradictions within the idealist position. At the same time, it integrates the purely theoretical field with the practical or concrete domains of the social, historical, moral, political, and aesthetic, yielding a truly comprehensive world view. By so doing, we pass beyond epistemology to being and beyond ideas to human life (Lonergan, 1967).

What is the status of these six (or potentially seven) levels? The best analogy is to the levels of early philosophical development described and illustrated by Piaget (1929). These were not stages but ideal-types. The definition of stages depends on the longitudinal pursuit of individual subjects through structural transformations of their understanding. However, it should be pointed out that such study (currently under way in the case of the work described here) may not be sufficient to demonstrate stages. While there may be cognitively more adequate problem-solving capacities at successive stages in the formally described domains of logic and moral judgment—domains where there are "answers"—naive epistemology and metaphysics may constitute less a realm of truth than of meaning. In such a case, development would amount to increasing the meaningfulness of interpretive scope of patterns and contents of belief, and would be manifest in the process of reasoning, rather than in the structural adequacy of cognition. Such possibilities are made cogent by Arendt's (1977) distinction between meaning and truth, reasoning and cognition.

Stage theories of the development of formal problem-solving rationality are not only individualistic but also intellectualist, obscuring their historical dimensions and pretending to independently generate new stages out of the logical contradictions inherent in previous stages. Levels of philosophical meaning as described here, conversely, are much more blatantly integrated with and dependent on collective sociohistorical forms of intellectual and political tradition. A concrete example is offered by the divided self of level 3. As I have argued elsewhere, such a psychological split is made possible by the historical separation of public and private in the sociological sphere, a division maintained intellectually in the nineteenth and twentieth centuries through the instrument of liberal ideology (Unger, 1975).

Finally, there remains the important question of how the levels of naive philosophy, here described abstractly, relate to the sphere of human practical activity. Some of these connections have already been made by Kohlberg and Gilligan (1971) and Chandler (1974), who suggest that the emergence of the "cogito" in early adolescence can explain such diverse adolescent experiences and activities as loneliness, gregariousness, self-consciousness, and the esthetic significance of dance, music and sex. Elsewhere, I have pointed to diverse cultural manifestations of natural philosophy such as "Star Trek" and the recent interest in cloning (Broughton, 1975b).

Jody, a high school senior, said that he felt true friendship was an impossibility because, however much people seemed to like each other and agree on things, there was always a difference between them. In manner, he was obsessively argumentative, opposing others as a matter of principle and always seeking differences between himself and others. He used his metaphysical position to explain away a recent split between him and his best friend. In the interview, he was consistently level 5, exercising to the limit the particularism and relativism of that philosophy. The correspondence between this level and his reflections on his personal life could have several different interpretations, of course. One issue raised by this example is the question of whether the intellectual levels could represent intellectualizations for some persons, which serve a primarily defensive function.

Another subject, Wade (see above), started to talk about the recent death of his father after the interview was finished, apparently in delayed response to questions about the mortality of the body. He desperately wanted to believe that his father's spirit was still alive in some sense. Yet while holding to a level 4 notion of self, he had doubts about the existence of an immortal soul. The grounds for rejecting the spiritual perspective were that "this was not plausible, not acceptable to many people." This young man's considerable confusion around his loss resulted from the inherent contradiction between his "substantial" conception of self and a conventional view of truth.

Other examples could be enumerated, especially in the mind/body category (which, as Baldwin [1906-11] suggested, appears to be central to adult thought). A young woman suffering from a usually terminal illness, talks about her sense of herself as riding in a tank. A young woman with personal problems talks about the gap between physical and mental love. A political prisoner talks about transcending physical pain through spiritual attitude. Whether these descriptions are modes of understanding imposed on experience, intellectual reflections abstracted from concrete practical actions, or both, remains to be investigated. The extent to which naive philosophies develop in response to individual introspection or emerge from collective thought and action also remains to be seen (Broughton, 1977b).

But one can say from present observational and anecdotal evidence that it is becoming increasingly improbable that reflective thought of the kind described here is a superfluous part of our mental and physical life. If it were, would so many be so involved in such a complex theoretical and practical labor as the study of "social cognition"? The attendant conceptual complexities discussed at the outset of this chapter are, after all, aspects of psychophysical and other dualisms, which plague the reflective thought not only of professional philosophers but of psychologists as well. It is the peculiar and ironic responsibility of a "genetic philosophy" that it must, at its higher stages, be able to account for the cognitive processes of its own creators and thereby justify its own possibility.

## references

Adorno, T. W., and others. *The Positivist Dispute in German Sciology.* New York: Harper & Row, 1976.

Baldwin, J.M. *Thought and Things.* 3 vols. London: Swann Sonnenschein, 1906-1911.

Blasi, A., and Hoeffel, E. C. "Adolescence and Formal Operations." *Human Development,* 1974, *17,* 344-363.

Broughton, J. M. "The Developmental Psychology of the Mind/Body Problem." In R. W. Rieber (Ed.), *Mind and Body.* New York: Academic Press, forthcoming.

Broughton, J. M. "The Impact of Social Structure on Development." In C. Cranford (Ed.), *The Study of Human Growth and Development.* Guildford, Conn.: Dushkin Publishing, forthcoming.

Broughton, J.M. "The Cognitive Development of Subject/Object Concepts." Paper presented at the annual meeting of the American Psychological Association, Chicago, August, 1975a.

Broughton, J.M. "The Development of Natural Epistemology in the Years 10-26." Unpublished doctoral dissertation, Harvard University, 1975b.

Broughton, J. M., and Freeman-Moir, J. D. *Foundations of Cognitive-Developmental Psychology.* New York: Johnson-Ablex, forthcoming.

Broughton, J. M., and Riegel, K. F. "Developmental Psychology and the Self." *Annals of the New York Academy of Science,* 1977, *291,* 149-167.

Cassirer, E. *Substance and Function.* New York: Dover, 1923.

Chandler, M. J. "Heating Up the Colder Side of Cognition." *Newsletter of the Society for Research in Child Development,* Summer, 1974.

Erikson, E. *Identity: Youth and Crisis.* New York: Norton, 1968.

Frondizi, R. *The Nature of the Self.* Carbondale: Southern Illinois Press, 1953.

Hall, G. S. *Adolescence.* 2 vols. New York: Appleton, 1904.

Harre, R., and Secord, P. *The Explanation of Social Behavior.* Totowa, N.J.: Rowman & Littlefield, 1972.

Inhelder, B., and Piaget, J. *The Growth of Logical Thinking from Childhood to Adolescence.* New York: Basic Books, 1958.

Kohlberg, L., and Gilligan, C. "The Adolescent as Philosopher." *Daedalus,* 1971, *100* 1051-1086.

Lonergan, B. J. F. "Cognitional Structure." In B. J. F. Lonergan (Ed.), *Collection Papers by B. J. F. Lonergan.* Montreal: Palm Publishers, 1967.

Merleau-Ponty, K. *The Structure of Behavior.* Boston: Beacon Press, 1963.

Piaget, J. *The Child's Conception of the World.* New York: Harcourt Brace Jovanovich, 1929.

Shantz, C. U. "The Development of Social Cognition." In E. M. Hetherington (Ed.), *Review of Child Development Research.* Vol. 5. Chicago: University of Chicago Press, 1975.

Sigel, I. "A Model of Developmental Person-Perception." Paper presented at the biennial meeting of the Society for Research in Child Development, Denver, April 1975.

Toulmin, S. E. "Rules and Their Relevance for Understanding Human Behavior." In *Review of Child Development Research.* Vol. 5. Chicago: University of Chicago Press, 1975.

Unger, R. M. *Knowledge and Politics.* New York: Free Press, 1975.

*John Broughton is assistant professor at Teachers College, Columbia University.*

*In the course of children's gradual construction of an*
*"objective" societal knowledge, one can witness*
*the very process of development at work.*

# children's societal understanding and the process of equilibration

## hans g. furth

Piaget (1932) noted that young children's conduct and conversation with adults are very different from their behavior toward peers. The main difference is clearly due to the children's disparate understanding of the rules underlying the two relations. In a child's relations with adults, it is a matter of submitting to adults or playing the role of a child according to rules that are externally impressed on children. Given the most favorable cases of parental upbringing, there are bound to be a vast number of situations when the behavior of the adults and the rules that children have to follow are, from children's viewpoints, simply incomprehensible and totally arbitrary. The strongest emotional convictions of acceptance and love receive occasional shocks when children exclaim, "Mom, if you won't let me do that, I will not be your best friend." We must not underestimate the intellectual conflict experienced by the child here, even though the emotional upheaval is probably quite fleeting and easily overcome by subsequent encounters of mutual positive affect. But intellectually it is not so different from what would happen if every now and then we observed that two plus three equaled six or that one hour after three o'clock the time was half past two.

In young children's interactions with adults, the situation is often one of inequality and unilateral respect. Again leaving aside the emotional relation that can be entirely positive and mutually loving, intellectually it is as difficult for the child to grasp the rules of adult social life as it is difficult for the adult to take childish notions seriously. The problems of adult psychology aside, children often deal with such difficulties just as they deal with other events that are of personal interest but are too far removed from adequate comprehension: through play. Children's play is one of equilibration's answers to problems that would cause unsolvable conflicts. The playful attitude provides children with a conflict-free world. They may be fascinated with the satisfaction-promising smell and activity of the kitchen and represent in play their understanding of the kitchen without having to be careful about burning, breaking, or any other constraint that a real kitchen implies. Or they may be motivated by emotional reasons to reenact symbolically the spanking of a naughty child, having full control of the rules governing misdeeds and punishment. Or again they may exhibit to imagined onlookers a feat of skillful performance that they know would not stand up to the review of real people.

The playful attitude is a healthy and psychologically sensible strategy to cope with a world that is beyond the reach of adequate comprehension. It selectively focuses on what can be understood and avoids having to deal with other points of view that could disturb the present intellectual balance. In this sense it illustrates precisely what Piaget described by the concept of egocentrism. What makes children's behavior "childish" to our judgment is their not taking things seriously and playing at them. Later sections of this chapter will return to children's play as one way in which equilibrium may deal with social interactions that are beyond the understanding of the child.

The relation between peers is often on a different footing. As young children play with each other, do things together, or hold a conversation, their interpersonal behavior is guided by rules that are to a great extent of their own making. The children themselves understand on their own terms what is going on, and their understanding is a direct result of their own activity in setting up and maintaining those interpersonal relations. In dealing with peers, children act as coequals and their construction of interpersonal relations is on a level of mutual respect. These are the very conditions that are favorable for intellectual development. Mutual respect implies a serious effort to take the other person's viewpoint into account. The inevitable clashes of opposing opinions, the striking out into new behavioral patterns, the recognition of unsuspected individual or common needs, become so many occasions for the equilibration process to act on and coordinate. Equilibration, the central regulating process in Piaget's developmental description (Piaget, 1977), does not only mean the restoring of a previous balance that was temporarily disturbed (as in the case of childhood play cited above). Equilibration is also an expanding process through which conflicts may be not only negatively avoided but also positively incorporated into a new balance. In the case of peer relations, the new balance could correspond to a new understanding of what a friend is, together with a more adequate concept of person and self.

Consequently, we should recognize that children's peer relations are bound to be more real and their relations to the adult world more playful. Sitting quietly next to dad on a bus is for the four-year-old girl a play that she chooses to enact—no doubt out of a mixture of love and fear (which are quite real to her), much as she would choose to enact the role of the bus driver when playing bus at home. In contrast, the girl's interactions with a friend, such as sharing an apple, helping the friend set up a toy, or pushing the friend to do something against his or her will, are for real: Here the two children are literally constructing their social life and fashioning themselves into socialized persons.

Whether between children and adults or between children and their peers, whether playful or serious, social interactions are ubiquitous in a child's life and predominant in a child's development. Why is it, then, that it was in their understanding of material things that Piaget observed children's first acquisition of logical thinking free of playful egocentrism? One answer, no doubt, is his and Western society's preoccupation with the scientific enterprise, where mathematical operations are predominant. In a different climate, one could have as easily singled out the children's evident maturity in their peer interactions. Indeed, as noted above, Piaget did observe with interest the contrast between the relatively mature peer interactions between children and their more unilateral and egocentric contact with the adult world. In this sense, the development of logical understanding may as readily be found in children's social interactions as in their conceptions of material things.

For Piaget, logic is the norm of reasonable discourse, primarily in the form of conversation between two or more equals, and derivatively in the private form of articulating for oneself (as in writing or simply in silent thinking). Discourse implies two distinct properties: a serious effort at communicating one's view, and a willingness to take seriously the other person's viewpoint and to coordinate it with one's own. A five-year-old boy may observe two events of breaking something — say, breaking off the pedal of a bicycle and breaking off a tree branch that served as a swing. To drive the point home, we imagine this boy to have been born profoundly deaf and as a consequence to be very much lacking in what he can communicate by means of society's language. We now assume that the boy accompanies his father to the bicycle shop where they buy a new pedal, which they then screw onto the bicycle. The boy, privately reflecting on the two events, now contrasts the repair of the bicycle with the tree shorn of its branch. This contrast is by itself an advanced intellectual attitude over a previously held playful confusion of living and made things. For this child, similar contrasts have occasioned some curious searchings over conflicting opinions. The present occasion, however, causes hardly a ripple but confirms something he has now suspected for some time: Some things, he says to himself, are made by people and can be repaired, other things grow from within and cannot.

Such an insight, together with a thousand other similar intellectual achievements, changes the child's reality considerably. We can call this a developmental experience (Piaget calls it a logical-mathematical experience), by which we refer to the process of expanding equilibration. This experience can be one that the child is reflectively aware of, or more frequently something that can only be inferred by close observation. We have described the present developmental experience to illustrate the similarity between a real discourse and the implicit discourse of a thinking person who compares and coordinates different viewpoints. This boy may never have been able to talk about his views to other people; however, the crucial thing for moving a child's mind from an egocentric playfulness to a socialized seriousness is not so much knowledge of syntax or vocabulary but the intellectual attitude that makes discourse possible.

The general coordinations of actions are for Piaget at the base of all logical understanding, physical as well as social. But in the life of human beings, personal and societal interactions are infinitely more important than mere interactions with things. The main goal of childhood is to benefit from existing society, learning about the physical world as a by-product of the larger task of becoming socialized. As a species we could not survive one generation if this were the other way around. Piaget saw in the intellectual egocentrism of symbol-forming intelligence a continuation — though diminished — of the self-satisfying tendency of a sensorimotor intelligence that knew neither self nor the other. Egocentrism recedes only in proportion to the person's more adequate separation of the subject and the object. This separation is only possible by means of logical instruments constructed by the person, and the primary external motivation for this construction — and hence for the development of logic itself — is the social environment to which the children are effectively and emotionally attached. The internal motivation is the equilibrating process of the intelligence, which through its own activity tends to expand and to coordinate the contributions afforded by the external (social and physical) and internal (biological and physiological) environment. The need to communicate, to share one's thinking with others, and to coordinate other people's with one's own thinking prepares this developmental process. Of its own momentum, the process then continues in the direction of social collaboration. Logic, therefore, is both subjective and social — not in the sense that it is individualistic or due to a social convention — but rather because it is the mental product of the socialized subject who takes account of what all other viewpoints have in common. "Logic is not isolated from life; it is no more than the expression of operational coordination essential to action" (Inhelder and Piaget, 1958, p. 342). In the cited work, Piaget refers specifically to the societal life of adolescents and to their changed personal interrelations.

### stages of understanding in the use of money

One hundred twenty-two boys and girls from southern England, ages five through eleven, were interviewed on their understanding of societal experiences, including their conceptions of government, community, and social institutions such as money. The children's responses were classified into four developmental stages along a continuum from stage 1 (playful images) to stage 4 (systematic understanding). Distribution of subjects across the four stages is shown in Table 1. Given the discussion in the previous section, it should come as no surprise that the youngest children at stage 1 initially oriented to our questions with a playful attitude. The stage 1 playful images were a natural response of young children to questions about social structures and institutions from the adult social world. Stages 2 and 3 were transitional; stage 2 was characterized by a functional understanding of per-

Table 1. Percent Distributions of Subjects Across
Stages of Conception of Buying and Selling ($N$ = 122)

| Developmental Stage | AGE | | | | | | |
|---|---|---|---|---|---|---|---|
| | 5 ($n=7$) | 6 ($n=28$) | 7 ($n=18$) | 8 ($n=16$) | 9 ($n=24$) | 10 ($n=21$) | 11 ($n=8$) |
| 1 | 100 | 61 | 22 | — | — | — | — |
| 2 | — | 25 | 33 | 56 | 29 | 14 | — |
| 3 | — | 14 | 44 | 38 | 67 | 62 | 63 |
| 4 | — | — | — | 6 | 4 | 24 | 37 |

Note. In stage 1, children describe monetary change as the main source of money and see goods as free to the shop. In stage 2, children do not relate their own paying for goods to the shopowner's paying. In stage 3, children consider the shopowner's own money as deriving from an extraneous source. In stage 4, the profit of the shopowner is described and understood.

sonal societal observations with little or no further interpretation; stage 3 was characterized by the construction of partial interpretations or theories that stopped short of being systematic and thus led to compromises, inconsistencies, and conflict. The two key areas in early societal understanding evolved around the child's understanding of the use of money and the distinction between personal and societal relating. In hindsight it seems obvious that these two areas of understanding are necessary before the more complex concepts of government and societal community develop. In fact, stage 4 is probably the equivalent of concrete societal understanding, after which one could expect a more adequate understanding in these more complex concepts.

While the next two sections will provide examples of the variety of children's images and thinking on many societal experiences, the stage concept can be illustrated by the children's understanding of the use of money in a retail store. In stage 1 the children do not understand at all the function of paying. They think of it as a ritual by which the customer gives money and in return gets goods and money change back. Many children considered the change as one's chief source of obtaining money. In stage 2 the function of paying and money change in its immediate context is understood, but beyond this there is no realization about the further use of the money. In stage 3 the connection between the customer's and the store's payment for goods is made. However, profit is not understood, and the shopowner's own expenses are thought to derive from an extraneous source. This logical inconsistency, characteristic of stage 3, is overcome in stage 4.

## developmental thinking about society

The developmental approach to societal understanding would be supported most directly if children's notions of societal institutions can be interpreted as developmental acquisitions. As was suggested above, developmental acquisitions result from the equilibration process, peculiar to intelligence, through which both subjective and objective coordinations are established, the former culminating in a thinking, socialized personality (self), the latter in a society of adult people with their objective reality. Our attempt to organize and interpret children's dialogues, recorded in our transcripts, revealed types of thinking that would be hard to explain through any but a developmental theory. Specifically, we noted that the children's ideas were original: They observed and interpreted societal events such as are never recorded by adults. Moreover, their ideas could hardly be called an inadequate knowing due to lack of information. It was not that they knew less but that they knew differently: Their approach to societal reality was different, just as they themselves were different from socialized adults.

A different approach to reality means a different mental framework. The concept of developmental stages is merely a convenient shortcut to express this structural difference. In addition to the originality and the qualitative differences of children's societal thinking, three further observations are even more directly related to the equilibration process, namely, developmental experiences, conflicting theories, and playfulness in thinking. All three imply the qualities that Piaget ascribes to all developmental processes: construction, which looks forward to objective reality and necessitates new coordinations, and compensation, which looks back at subjective reality and overcomes internal conflicts. We shall first focus on these three types of thinking, and then discuss stages in relation to equilibration.

## developmental experiences and spontaneous opinions

Developmental experiences relate to an expanding framework of thinking and eventually lead to a more adequate understanding of observed events. When children (1) spontaneously express questions, often following these questions with original answers, (2) spontaneously correct themselves, or (3) express hesitation and discontent about a problem and subsequently solve it to their obvious satisfaction, one can be fairly sure that these activities are forms of active thinking that constitute developmental experiences. Susan (age five) wonders: *How he gets the same money when nobody's buyed it? . . . How does he get the money when nobody's buyed it? . . . How does he get the money who hasn't gaved him no money? How can he get it?* Joan (age six) does likewise: *Mm, because all people have money without getting it—where do they get it from?* Joan answers her question immediately: *They get it from when they were a child probably, they have pocket money, I have pocket money, and they'd saved it up and had some money.* Susan, too, replies on her own after some digression: *He makes the money, the money, who made it . . . the people who made it, they go with their money, with their car or lorry to buy it, to give the shopkeeper.*

Don (age six) on numerous occasions shows spontaneous corrections and other forms of active thinking:

(What sort of people would become a bus conductor?) *Boys, not girls.* (Not girls?) *Girls can be bus conductors, but they can't be bus drivers.* (Why can't they be drivers?) *Well, they can be drivers. . . .* (And is he still a bus driver when he's at home?) *Yes, they never give up.* (Never?) *Once they choose and have to do it.* (Yes, They just go on, until when?) *Well, until the end of their life.* (What happens to the bus?) *Well perhaps it's still all right and someone else can choose it.*

The following day Don continues talking of the bus:

*People give* [tickets] *to the driver and pay him . . . and the bus conductor takes it and pays them some money back, not the money back that was paid them, just pays them some more* [that is, different money]. (What does he pay them?) *I don't know . . . and then, if they give a lot of money, the driver can give half to the conductor and half for him . . . keep it and buy things for him.*

Now two or three suggestive questions are going to lead to developmental experience for Don.

(Who buys the petrol?) *The bus driver.* (Where does he get the money for the petrol?) *The petrol man, he gives them petrol.* [This is the familiar idea of change as a source of money.] (Oh, why does the petrol man give him money?) *Oh,*

*no, the man gives him money. . . . Oh, I get it. The driver—
the people who go on the bus give the money to the people—the
people who go on the bus give the money to the man and then
the man can buy petrol.*

Don concludes this new insight with a general statement about the
source of money, *their own money, they save it up, they find a work,
they find a thing to do and then they get money.* This illustrates equilibration in action. First there is a playful attitude toward societal events
that cannot be understood, but even here there is an effort to follow
some logical rules. Then there is a willingness to consider another viewpoint, hence Don's corrections. Finally, there is a coordination of conflicting viewpoints and a construction of a new insight through which
the conflict is resolved.

These processes are also present in Anita. This seven-year-old
girl clearly expresses her internal discontent: *Well, I'm not very good
at knowing what they—how you get money.* After being questioned
about payment in the factory, she muses, *I think it's sort of like just me
walking into a shop to buy something. I think they have to buy the
stuff.* Asked further about money, she exclaims excitedly, *Why, I know
that one—from the money that they get from the people who walk into
the shop every day.*

At times children understand enough to reject an opinion that
they may have entertained earlier, but not quite enough to give a
totally adequate reply. Jeannie (age six) speaks of the necessity of training to become a teacher: *'Cuz you couldn't just go to school and say,
have you a job? Because you wouldn't know what to do, would you?
. . . They have to go to a special class first. . . . They don't do it in
school, they do it somewhere else. . . . It's just like driving lessons,
they don't have it* [the lessons] *in the garage, do they?* What Jeannie
rejects as silly is precisely how other children think about acquiring a
role. In another place, Jeannie presents several playful alternatives to
payment for teachers, but adds that the money for them does not come
"from the factories," an opinion that Susan actually does espouse as a
viable solution to the problem of how individuals acquire money.

### conflicting and reluctant thinking

In many cases one may observe how the various ideas that a
child holds are in logical conflict with each other, temporarily leading
to a dead end. In these and other cases, one can almost feel the obsta-

cles that operate within a child who is pursuing a logical direction that alters the child's habitual mode of thinking. Conflicting and reluctant thinking are the two signposts of transitional stages and were found most frequently in children classified as stage 3 in their societal thinking.

Take one child's (Sally, age nine) confusion about who gives money to whom in connection with the store, the factory, and the Council (local government), even though she is socially quite alert: *I'm interested to find out that. . . . I don't know any of them—who gets paid and who doesn't.* Alternately, Sally thinks: (1) The shop pays for the food and gets money from the Council; (2) the shop gets food from the Council; (3) the Council gives money to the factory to make food; (4) money collected from the customers goes to the shop workers; and (5) some of the money goes to the factory. She also thinks people do jobs without pay if they do something that they really want to do, *like rock climbing.* But she continues, *Only you do get paid sometimes if you really wanted to get the money for something,* and she refers to the purchase of a house and a loan. In other words, she spontaneously uses her own criterion for nonpayment to illustrate a situation where payment occurs.

Roger (age eight) has ideas about the money paid to and by the shopkeeper that go in so many different directions that it is hard to follow his discourse: (1) The shopkeeper pays the factory from the collection of a money box. (2) The customer's money stays in the till. (3) Prodded on what happens to the money, Roger says, *They either share it out for themselves and give the people who gave them the stock some, for how much they had, like bananas, pears, and oranges, and they cost nine pounds for the pears and oranges and eleven pounds for the bananas.* (4) Some of the shop's money goes to old people, pensioners, *and lifeboat people, for instance . . . and some to the fire engine.* (5) Regarding industry, Roger believes that each company has two parts: the "actual" company and the workers. (6) He explains how the company functions: *Something like this—two companies, and one owns a housing estate and the other company is a road company . . . one builds a house, they earn money for it, from the road company for building them and then the road company . . . that's how they earn money, money from each other.* (7) The main source of money is saving by collecting money in a money box.

Related to conflicting thinking, or rather to the child's wish to avoid it, are essentially stable compromise solutions that we call reluctant thinking. One example is Sam (age nine) when he suggests that the Council's money derives from their work: *I would imagine that they would have to work. . . . They have to get a lot of money so that I ima-gine they work in a factory.* Furthermore, *the town pays them, some-how.* And with this "somehow," he has come to a dead end. Denise (age ten) uses a common solution to the problem of personal money for the shopowner: *Well, if there is any money left over, he can have that, and if he did the shopping in the mornings, and during his lunch hour he went and did another shopping, he'd get a lot of money.* Sarah (age eleven) goes one step further by expressing a reluctance to letting shop money be used for the personal needs of the shopowner: *I think they would get it out like any normal person would, when they are not actu-ally in the shop, when they're actually in their own home, because you can't really take the money out of the till. . . . Like an ordinary fam-ily, like mine, when you get money out of the bank and out of the tin.*

## playful images

In this section we consider a few of the many instances when the children seem not to take the interview seriously, producing comments that make us wish to ask the child, "Do you really believe this?" Two reasons can be proposed for taking these comments at face value. First, seriousness and playfulness are not clearly separate spheres of reality for the children. We will point out in the next section to what extent children's playing fits into the equilibration model of development. Second, in every play situation of pretend there is a core of thinking for real, and this is what we wish briefly to document first.

When Robert (age five) talks about the *fireman with a ride on the bus, he gets paid by the man standing in the back there,* we can well imagine this five-year-old boy at "real" play. The conductor on the bus who collects all the money—*the richest man in town,* one child called him—is seen as the source of money. Moreover, the conductor's and the fireman's activities are similar in that both move around on a motor car, and this similarity is expressed in Robert's image, in which the two roles are confused. Sally (age five) rejects the hypothetical situation where a mother can be a teacher (in play there is no hypothetical situation): *No . . . if teachers are teachers they can't be mothers, or if big ladies go to school that means they are teachers.* She then places the roles of her "toy" world in quite serious proper order: *Teachers be friends to mothers and man teachers be friends to mans . . . and chil-dren be friends to children and babies be friends to babies.* Christine (age six) is impressed by the restricted movements of telephones and comments spontaneously, *When we move, you see, mummy wants to take them. I say, you can't take them . . . 'cos we've got quite a few and they're all plugged together and when we take one out, they'll all fall over.* In her Humpty Dumpty world, some nice friends will provide the new telephones: *When we move, daddy's going to get one. If one of his friends has got quite a few, he'll probably give it to him.* Dad may have to pay for it, *but only one penny.* Sharing among friends is quite real to Christine. There is nothing playful about Grant's (age six) description of finding money, even though to us it may seem so: *Like my friends, the workers, well, when Geoffrey and my other mates who are here, they found lots of ten pences in the mud that they dug up and they found some every day when they were working except Sunday, and till they get more and more, they can own a shop.*

## developmental stages and equilibration

Equilibration means that children work out a balance between the worldly interactions that they observe and their underlying understanding. This understanding is partly a function of past development and experience and, particularly if it is a new event, partly a compensation responsive to the particular event. If the event is far removed from their experience, the compensation may take the extreme form of denial: Children, for instance, who hold that change is the source of a person's money, may simply not observe the occasions when no change is given. Another form of compensation is to deal with the event in a playful manner; that is, children may selectively focus on a few positive components of the event and use them according to personal interest and meaning without a serious effort of coherent understanding. Societal thinking of stage 1 was found to have this characteristic of imaginative playfulness.

At other times the compensation takes the form of a search for logical coherence. As a consequence two things happen. First, children begin more systematically to take note of what actually occurs and of conditions that modify the event. Second, children become more conscious of the theories that guide their thinking, both with respect to their subjective understanding and with respect to what they objectively attribute to the event. We have now two components as part of the equilibration process through which meaningful contact between person and environment is established: the observation of the event and of the child's interaction with the event, and the theoretical framework that guides the child's thinking and interprets the objective event.

equilib: obs. of the event, +
of the child's interaction w. it., +
his guiding theory

These two components mutually interact and influence each other. Equilibration means not merely that they are kept in a balance that is constantly active (insofar as these two components are in constant flux and open to change) but also that the interplay of these two components becomes the crucial occasion on which the child's general understanding is expanded in the direction of greater logical coherence and objective understanding. In other words, equilibration is the source of what we have earlier called developmental experiences. In connection with societal understanding, we have documented the variety and originality of active thinking and different forms of developmental experiences, particularly during the transitional stages 2 and 3. What remains is to analyze more clearly the interplay of these components and the origin and nature of those changes that lead to development. At the same time, this attempt to describe developmental changes should deepen the perhaps too superficial meaning commonly ascribed to stages.

We start with an interaction observed by children, using the concrete example of a small store. The children experience the store as a place that has all kinds of goods (and goodies for themselves) and that hands the goods over in response to a certain behavior. Of course children already have some vague ideas about what they can call their own and what is not their own and must not be touched. Also they have been given personal gifts and may have engaged in some exchange with their peers. Now they experience what seems to them a special kind of exchange: The shopkeeper gives you goods in exchange for money, and to complicate matters the transaction nearly always involves some change. As a consequence, the children observe their own actions as giving money, and they observe the result of their action as getting goods and money in return. The theoretical framework that they understand and apply to the event is their vague notion of gifts and personal exchange. Their thinking about shopping is playful since they do not comprehend the most basic function of money as a means of turning this transaction into a nonpersonal, that is, societal, exchange. This playfulness is a compensation: It permits them to think about shopping with all its interesting happenings and personal satisfactions without experiencing any conflict—indeed, without any need to search for a logical coherence behind these interactions.

This playfulness is the main characteristic of stage 1 societal thinking and decreases gradually until it practically disappears in stage 4. It corresponds to what Piaget has called egocentrism, that is, the assimilation of the world to the children's personal perspective without too much regard for other viewpoints that could conceivably disturb the balance between understanding and experience. In the preceding section we have focused on the serious thinking that forms the positive part of all genuine play. The negative part, as it were, concerns the lack of serious logical engagement apart from an immediate personal perspective or wish. Thus for Jim (age six) the bus driver just goes where he wants; for Grant (age six) *sometimes they don't want to take you and sometimes they do.* Similarly for Jessica (age six), the shopkeeper acquires a shop *because they want to be a shopkeeper, so they go to a place where a man tells you what you—if you can do it or you can't,* and Sally (age seven), while understanding the function of change, justifies her lack of concern about the use of the customers' money by the same playful attitude of a personal wish: *The wanted to do a shop, so they don't have to pay it.*

Given the children's present playful attitude, what processes disturb the actual balance and lead to development? Which of the two components mentioned act as the leading cause? It would seem that the children's general theoretical understanding here is the prime mover. As the children begin to understand numbers and quanitification, they develop a framework that they can apply to the use of money. As a result, what they observe is no longer the shopkeeper's giving of two things in exchange for money (namely, goods and money); instead the shopkeeper's giving of money comes to be regarded as an entirely different and altogether secondary behavior in comparison with the principal event of the giving of goods in exchange for the customer's money. Moreover, the customers' or the children's own behavior of giving money is now observed in greater detail. Generally, if one gives more money, one gets more goods of a given kind. But the price of the goods is not systematically related to the size, the weight, or the appearance of the money; change is not given unless one hands the shopkeeper more money than is asked; and the price of goods may be different in different stores. What the children have earlier neglected to notice as part of the ongoing interaction becomes comprehensible and thus part of their observed experience. Piaget suggests that the one-sided emphasis of the positively observed event may be a primary occasion for a potential disruption of the thinking balance. We might add that only when children take note of negative aspects of an event, of what an event is not, can they actually reach a more stable new balance. Many of the observations listed above deal with negative aspects: amount of money and the return of change is not related to the giving of goods.

Children whose thinking demonstrates the characteristics of the preceding paragraph are classified as stage 2. In addition to this objective understanding of money change and the diminished personalization of societal interactions, children at stage 2 elaborate notions which have a playful quality as soon as they venture beyond the immediately observed event. The most obvious indication of this limitation is their lack of associating the customer's paying for goods with the shopkeeper's paying for them.

To associate these two acts requires the construction of a societal system in which the shopkeeper is seen as a middle man between producer and consumer. Again we ask ourselves, what motivates children to interpret beyond observed events and construct systems? It would be difficult to point to any particular environmental experience. Rather it must be the children's realization that there are two areas of interactions governed by different rules: the personal area of being within a family and having friends, and the impersonal world of grownups with its money and articulated rules. Therefore, it is no longer sufficient for an understanding of what a shopkeeper does to refer to his or her personal wish or to the satisfaction of his or her own needs, just as it is no longer sufficient for the maintenance of a friendship to share some activity. The shopkeeper is placed into a societal system of buying and selling, and friends are considered within a personal system of similar personal tastes and interests. The construction of systems is a slow process with its own peculiar difficulties in that one part-system may clash with another part-system or be inadequate to explain more than the obvious components of observed events. So it is again the children's own theoretical framework that guides their explorations into a more systematic understanding of how people within society interact. Those children showing stage 3 societal thinking provide a great number of concrete instances of constructing part-theories or, as demonstrated in the section "Developmental Experiences and Spontaneous Opinions" above, often produce compromises and conflicts that are bound to disrupt the thinking balance.

We call compromise a temporarily stable solution to what is seen by the children as a problem, but which will turn out, once they reach the adequate insight, to be no problem at all. The most striking example of a compromise solution is the refusal to let the shopowner partake of the money collected in the till. This shows again how difficult it is for children to overcome the pull of the positive observation — in this case, the preoccupation with the till and its exclusive use for the business.

In stage 4 of societal understanding, we observed a mode of thinking that is radically different from the playful mode predominant in stages 1 and 2 and still present in stage 3. It would be foolish to maintain that it disappears entirely. Pockets of childlike playfulness are found in the minds of the most advanced adults. However, adults know the difference between serious efforts at understanding and playful imaginings, particularly in areas that the society values as obviously real (such as the economic or the political-legal system). It is striking that at stage 4 all kinds of previous problems, conflicts, and compromises fall into place or simply disappear. It is no longer important to observe whether the customers pay their money to one or the other cashier; the till is a mere secondary convenience, and some personal money for the shopowner out of the customer's money is considered an obvious consequence of the system. These obvious gains in societal understanding come about through a gradual accumulation and coordination of small developmental experiences and different forms of active thinking.

It is probably not coincidental that the few children who appeared mature in understanding individual differences in personal and societal roles were also among those few who regarded profit as part of business, finding it obvious that the shopowner should be paid more for the goods than he had paid in order to have money for his personal needs. The basic economic understanding was the main criterion for stage 4 societal thinking. In terms of the schema proposed at the beginning of this section, these children's observations of what takes place when buying something in a store are bound to be very different from those of children of less advanced societal thinking. The child now knows how to move from the personal to the societal use of money and back again, regarding the transaction in this reversible manner, rather than as a simple transfer of ownership. In buying something, the personal money of the customer becomes societal money as part of the business, and this in turn includes the component of profit, which then returns to personal use.

If one looks for a correspondence to Piaget's operatory stages, it seems fairly obvious that only stage 4 shows characteristics of consistent and reversible thinking that could be referred to as societal operations. In the societal-personal field, the concrete-formal distinction does not seem applicable at all. Rather, in line with the theory outlined in the final section and some empirical evidence from the development of political thinking in adolescents (Adelson, 1971; Connell, 1971), one can expect that the major expansions of societal understanding in terms of a community and body politic begins *after* the achievement of stage 4 which serves as a necessary base. For this reason we have called stage 4 "concrete-systemic." This means that the children's thinking is systematic and therefore free of major internal inconsistencies, but it is limited in its scope to the systematic understanding of observed societal relations. As suggested in the following section, adolescents increasingly experience the subjective components of their lives as autonomous, that is, free from external reality. On the one hand they construct a differentiated psychological framework of self (their personality) and others (personal and societal relations), and on the other hand they can engage in the formal mode of thinking. These components interact as subjective and objective theories in an ongoing response to subjective and objective actions (experiences). The same equilibrating force that coordinated these components at earlier levels operates and probably leads to a more advanced stage of societal thinking that could be called systemic-analytic. Its distinguishing characteristic would be a formal-general rather than a personal-particular approach to societal events. One could expect a grasp of historical time and of political considerations, and an appreciation of the social community as an equilibrated totality that results from people's cooperation. In any case, social-personal and social-societal development would be interrelated so that the more advanced understanding of self and others is both a result and a cause of a more analytic understanding of society.

### knowledge as a relation

Piaget discovered the source of abstract categories of thinking in the sensorimotor coordinations of the preverbal infant. These coordinations establish a relation of knowing between the infant and the world and are observed as interactions between persons and objects. The interaction is both dialectic and productive: dialectic because there is both incoming assimilation of content to psychological schemes of action and outgoing accommodation (or adjustment) of the schemes to the individual content of the action, and productive because the interactions result in the experience of observed "objects," in the form of observations, and of a knowing "subject," in the form of mental frameworks. Piaget described the overall regulation of these interactions as the process of equilibration, which not only maintains a "productive" balance but also an "expanding" balance between knower and known. Schemes are the internal psychological capacities of organizing the interactions and differ in structure and complexity as children develop from infancy to adulthood. Piaget has described the growth of the schemes under the technical name of development in stages, from reflex schemes to sensorimotor coordinations, and beyond the latter to the "object" scheme, representations (symbols), and finally operations.

It is customary to list four developmental stages: sensorimotor, preoperatory, concrete, and formal operations. Sensorimotor interactions are coordinations of actions in the presence of the objects. Preoperatory interactions start when children can separate their interactions from the objects so that the object becomes as thing-that-is-known, even in its absence. At the same time, children begin to experience themselves as a self-that-knows, or as one among many people. In contrast to sensorimotor functioning, in which infants live in a perceptually present world, the reality of this preoperatory world is radically extended in the form of objects (concepts) and representations (images, language, and play). But this reality is still self-focused and logically confusing to the extent that the children do not yet have a framework of objectifying the concepts and representations. Theirs is a subjective, playful world in which there is no objective, logical necessity. It is operations that provide the systems of transformations that result in the experience and knowledge of logical necessity. In concrete operations this experience is still limited to interactions that can be concretely imagined; logic and what is physically real are too closely identified. Formal operations imply this further separation between reality and what is logically possible or necessary, so that the real is now experienced as one among other theoretical possibilities.

The gist of this summary description is a view of development as a construction on the part of growing children through which they acquire the framework for organizing the world. As the framework changes, so do the children and their reality. The radical constructionism of Piaget becomes apparent in that the most objective knowledge is the product of the most advanced subjective schemes and that a subjective knowledge component is present in all behavior, not merely in the restricted area of theoretical and verbal knowledge. The theory shows that the structure of all theoretical and verbal knowledge derives from the general coordinations of actions, and at all levels this structure retains its action (and interactional) character. If this is the case, then any human product—whether it is something made, like a chair; something imagined, like a symphony; or some enterprise, like a family—necessarily bears a close relation to the basic schemes of knowing that organized the actions in the first place.

Piaget's developmental theory of knowledge seems on the surface to deal almost exclusively with the general mental framework governing only one special form of human knowledge, namely, logical-mathematical and scientific thinking. Even if one accepts this form of thinking as quite special on account of its explicit object to attain "objective truth," one perhaps would not attempt to link the development of this knowledge to the development of other forms of behavior, particularly social behavior—unless one could establish a deep perspective. This relation is implicitly assumed and on occasions spelled out, though never in sufficient detail to outweigh the sheer bulk and emphasis of his research on strictly logical thinking.

Children are born into the social world, and their main task is to become socialized in the sense of becoming part of the adult world. With this as the primary purpose of development, the development of logical reason can almost be thought of as a corollary, even though in actual fact this is a chicken-and-egg question. However, one reason why Piaget's theory has been relegated to a psychology of the individual thinker is the lack of realization of the profound relation between logic and society. Logic, it was said above, derives from the general coordinations of actions; in other words, it relates to what is general and common. This is true in several respects: First, all external actions are directly or indirectly social and consequently their coordinations relate one to another person. Second, the need to verify and to question one's own ideas does not arise spontaneously from one's own solitary thinking or even from any contradictory environmental experience. (History testifies how tenaciously opinions can be maintained in the face of overwhelming contrary evidence: "Things are in the wrong, not the opinions.") Rather, the need arises when there is a genuine desire to coordinate one's own with others' viewpoints, when there is true communication about a problem to be solved. Third, logic is what all viewpoints have in common, such that two plus three equals five to any reasonable person of whatever culture or societal or personal condition. In the final analysis, the operations (in Piaget's sense) that provide a stable structure to our personal mental life are the same that make stable cooperation (the constructive relating of people) possible.

In this perspective, to develop logically means to develop socially—and vice versa. For children to communicate means for them to relate their own thinking to the thinking of others, and this becomes the primary occasion for development. Often this communication disrupts a previously held subject-object balance and creates an internal disturbance. Development consists in the construction of a new balance to compensate for the disturbance. The new balance does not merely restore a previous state (in which case there would be no development and no genuine construction) but moves the children's total intelligence toward a higher stage. Piaget calls this a process of expanding equilibration and considers it to be the principal motor of development, intrinsic to human intelligence.

Equilibration gives substance to a constructivist approach to the human mind and its products. The social world is certainly one of the principal products, and it is the obligatory environment in which children grow up to develop an adult, socialized mind. Piaget's own work focused on the structure of thinking. For that reason he studied the general coordinations of sensorimotor actions and the general, logical structures that ensure logical truth in reasoning, namely, logical and mathematical categories. As soon as one focuses on a particular content area, one deals with many factors extraneous to logic. But — and this is one of Piaget's main contentions — some form of logic (or prelogic?) influences all forms of human behavior, and social interactions are recognized to be the main content area of all development. The rules of social interactions form a logic (even though we do not adequately understand it), which logicians may find uninteresting. This logic underlies the coherence of a social group as well as the coherence of a personal self. Due to ever present personal-emotional components, this coherence is not a logically perfect system but is always relative and imperfect. Nevertheless, there is a reasonable equilibration at work that maintains societies and personal relations, and this equilibration in social interactions is the same process as the one that moves a child's mind to the understanding of logical and mathematical categories.

Societal institutions are midway between physical phenomena (for example, weight) and personal relations (for example, friendship) in that they present themselves to adults as objectively given, with some clear-cut rules of how they work. Adults could easily recognize a list of statements relative to business, occupational roles, government, or community that express the logical framework peculiar to these institutions. To understand societal institutions means precisely to understand this framework. The developmental approach assumes that the acquisition of this framework is in part a developmental process and will depend on the child's general stage of development. In particular, one could expect that children's thinking about society will show characteristics common to all serious efforts at making sense of the world: There will be a first period of self-centered playfulness when reality (what adults call real) and imagination are poorly differentiated. During a transition period toward an objective societal knowledge, the children's observations of societal events and their theoretical interpretations (frameworks) will be progressively interrelated and coordinated with general principles of reasoning. It is during this transitional period that one could observe evidence for equilibration at work: internal conflicts, logical compromises, developmental insights, conceptual difficulties, and misunderstandings and distortions of things heard and learned. One could also expect that societal understanding will lag behind the understanding of some concrete situations because societal institutions are not really concrete things but systems of interrelations that balance individual with community needs, the present with the past and the future, the concrete happening with what is theoretically possible.

Moreover, developmental theory would also predict that societal understanding will have its repercussions on personal-social understanding. In fact, one could be tempted to assume that understanding of personal relations comes long before understanding of societal relations. After all, children relate to adults and peers rather successfully at a time when there is no question of any societal understanding. It is, however, possible to distinguish between a sensorimotor and emotional relating that reaches back to the earliest infancy and prelogical (egocentric) forms of relating associated either with assimilative playfulness and no serious effort at adaptive accommodation or with a submissive accommodation of adult-instigated relations that does not corespond to an adequate assimilation. In between these two poles of unbalanced play and submission relations there are ongoing interactions between the child and other persons and things where vigorous assimilation and accommodation are in an even balance. This is conspicuously the case when children spontaneously explore their powers of action and understanding by testing the responsiveness of various things (for example, a wooden block as an occasion for lifting, feeling weight, crushing, standing on, building, and so on) and by testing the interrelations with their peers (for example, playing, sharing, turn taking, persuading, and saving face).

Piaget holds that a genuine understanding of what a person (or a self) is, is closely related to two psychological attitudes that he considers to correlate with formal thinking: the experience of the self as an autonomous thinker and of reality as grounded in a theoretical framework. From these follow the possibility of an adequate understanding and being a part of adult society, insofar as societal institutions are abstract entities for balancing a multitude of personal, economical, poli-

122

tical, and historical-traditional interrelations. In short, the social content of the child's world would contain within itself three social interrelations that, with development, become progressively differentiated: the self, other people, and society.

## references

Adelson, J. "The Political Imagination of the Young Adolescent." *Daedalus,* 1971, *100,* 1013-1050.

Connell, R. W. *The Child's Construction of Politics.* Melbourne, Australia: Melbourne University Press, 1971.

Inhelder, B., and Piaget, J. *The Growth of Logical Thinking from Childhood to Adolescence.* New York: Basic Books, 1958.

Piaget, J. *The Development of Thought.* New York: Viking Press, 1977.

Piaget, J. *The Moral Judgement of the Child.* New York: Harcourt Press, 1932.

*Hans G. Furth is professor of psychology at the
Boys Town Center, Catholic University,
Washington, D.C.*

*This review of the literature on social cognition indicates considerable recent progress. However, important issues remain unresolved in the conceptualization of skills and knowledge required for social understanding.*

# recent research on children's social cognition: a brief review

## david forbes

In light of the paramount importance of social understanding to the lives of both child and adult, it is ironic that the lion's share of psychologists' efforts has neglected the social domain in the study of human capacities for understanding. Perhaps the relative ease with which one may represent the physical world in the laboratory accounts in part for this neglect. Perhaps the neglect also reflects an inclination among scientific researchers to study mainly those kinds of understandings — the logical and physical — that are most in use during the workday of the scientist. In any case, the last decade and a half have seen concerted psychological research efforts toward the remediation of neglect concerning social cognition. A glance through recent psychological abstracts suggests that this area of inquiry is a rapidly growing one, with particular attention being paid to children and the development of social understanding.

### background

Fortunately, students of social-cognitive development need not begin entirely anew. The study of scientific thinking and of children's

logical and physical conceptions, most notably by Piaget and his fol-
lowers, has provided a considerable base, both in theoretical models
and in methodological insights for the study of intellectual development. In addition, there is a considerable body of philosophical theory
regarding social processes and their relation to intelligence — a legacy
from psychologically oriented writers such as James Mark Baldwin
(1906) and George Herbert Mead (1934).

Work on children's scientific thinking has relied on a few broad
assumptions about the nature of intellectual development. Most generally stated they are:

1. Children's conceptions about the world are best viewed as
consisting of organized "knowledge systems," whose character, albeit
different from that of adults, is no less describable by reference to formal models.

2. Development entails a series of qualitative transformations
in the nature of these systems, with more flexible and adaptive systems
replacing primitive ones.

3. The knowledge systems that children possess partly determine their understanding of and responses to events. Conversely, out-
comes resulting from contact between primitive knowledge systems and
the world will promote change in the knowledge system, making it also
in some sense determined by the experience of the child.

Piaget's work has also supplied social-cognitive research with
one widely adopted way of characterizing the thought of young
children. This is the concept of egocentrism, which refers to an
inability to free oneself from one's own particular subjective view of
events. Piaget originally discussed egocentrism in his studies of child
language and communication. Here he found that a major impedi-
ment to effective communication in childhood was the child's tendency to confuse his or her own knowledge with that of the other, and
consequently to ignore the other's informational needs. One particular
line of research that derives from the concept of egocentrism directly
relates to social-cognitive research. Inhelder and Piaget (1956) report
a series of investigations of children's ability to examine a visual array
of objects (such as an arrangement of three mountains) and to determine how these would appear to someone who viewed them from a different position. Piaget found that prior to about six years, the young
child egocentrically attributes the view of the self to the other. By age
six or seven, the child comes to recognize that something is different
about the viewpoint of the other but encounters considerable difficulty
in specifying the differences. Finally, by age eight or nine, the child is

able to coordinate the spatial view of self and other and to precisely reconstruct the other's view.

Subsequent investigation into spatial perspective taking has modified Piaget's original finding and provides more detail about the nature of children's waning egocentrism. Flavell (1974), in a recent review of this work, suggests that two accomplishments may be discriminated in the child's performance of this task: recognizing that the other indeed *has* a perspective different from that of the self, and specifying exactly what this perspective might be. The first of these two accomplishments is directly relevant to the student of social cognition, signalling a decreasing egocentrism in the child's concept of other persons that may, in some contexts, occur at as young an age as three years. The second relies more on the child's spatial manipulative ability and is less social in character. The child's inference of visual perspectives is therefore not equivalent in all aspects to true "social understanding." Still, childhood egocentrism, even when manifest in a relatively nonsocial context, bears important implications for social-cognitive research; particularly since the inverse of egocentrism, the recognition of one's own subjectivity and the ability to transcend this subjectivity, is central to the development of social understanding.

The work of Mead on the nature of social interaction also has aided social-cognitive research by providing the following two general propositions:

1. A fundamental feature of understanding other persons is a process whereby one takes the role of the other, thinking about the reactions that one's own actions will elicit from the other. The child is not born with the ability to take the other's role but must acquire this ability with development.

2. The process of developing social understanding goes beyond simply taking the role of others. It also entails the creation of generalized expectations about other's responses to self's actions, or the construction of a "generalized other."

### contemporary literature

In Mead's distinction of two types of role taking (vis a vis individual persons and the generalized other) he asserts that the first occurs with specific others during specific ongoing social interactions, whereas the second entails judgements about persons in general and occurs in the absence of a specific behavioral context. Gage and Cronbach (1955) expand on Mead's distinction, proposing five types of predictions that one might make in the course of a role-taking task. These are: (1) how *persons in general* will behave, (2) how a *particular category of persons* deviates from the behavior of persons in general, (3) how a *particular group* deviates from the typical behavior of the particular category to which it belongs, (4) how an *individual* deviates from the typical behavior of the particular group to which he belongs, and (5) how an individual on a *particular occasion* will deviate from his typical behavior.

In organizing this review, I propose that all role-taking activity (and in Mead's sense all social cognition) may be classified into one of three types. These types derive in part from Mead's distinction of particular and generalized others, but divide the former role-taking activity into two types, based on Gage and Cronbach's (1955) distinction between typical and particular behavior. The first type of role taking I shall call "taking the role of specific persons-in-contexts." The second will be called "taking the role of usual persons." The third received Mead's name, "taking the role of the generalized other." Taking the role of specific persons-in-contexts occurs when one actually interacts with another individual, relying on current information about the other's actions during the social encounter. Accordingly, the cognitive activity characteristic of this type of role taking is interpretation of others' significant social gestures. Taking the role of the usual person differs from the first type, relying mainly on experience with or general knowledge about the other. The cognitive activity characteristic of this type of role taking is identification of others' traits or behavioral tendencies, with consequent prediction of others' actions in the future. Taking the role of the generalized other relies on conceptions of social roles, institutions, and regulations rather than on any type of information specific to a particular other. The characteristic activity of this type of role taking is the construction of general expectations about human behavior based on knowledge about universally applicable facts of social interactions.

These three types of role-taking activity do not all occur independently. Rather, one should view them as a nested collection of activities: The first type almost always takes place in conjunction with the second and third, the second is almost always combined with the third, and only the third occurs by itself. Thus, when one is engaged in an actual interaction with another, one makes use of current information about the other, of information about how the other usually behaves (if one has it), and also of general social-psychological information applicable to all persons. Similarly, when one makes predictions about another's behavior, one considers how he or she usually behaves and also relies on information about how people in general behave. Only in speculations about how the anonymous one behaves does a person engage in a single, generalized type of role taking.

In addition to discussing the literature below as it pertains to these three types of role-taking activity, I shall also rely on one further distinction presented by Flavell (1968), who distinguishes studies of role-taking *accuracy* from studies of the role-taking *act*. The former measure the child's ability to take the role of another in varying contexts and with a variety of others, and such studies focus on the effects of context and other's characteristics on role-taking ability. The latter studies investigate the child's very attempt to create a mental relation between self and other. Analyses in these studies ignore variation in the child's success across various contexts and characteristics of other, focusing rather on the formal organization of the child's role-taking efforts.

The incorporation of Flavell's distinction into our taxonomy of foci for research leaves us with four categories of literature. I shall begin with literature deriving from Flavell's notion of "role taking as act" and then proceed through the literature pertinent to each of the three types of role taking where accuracy becomes an issue: taking the role of specific persons-in-context, taking the role of usual persons, and constructing the generalized other. I should point out that the section pertaining to the generalized other includes a variety of literature on children's knowledge of social relations, social institutions, and social regulations as well as on children's understanding of psychological concepts that apply to all persons. Much of this work has not been conceptualized by its authors as the study of role taking in any form, and in fact considerable debate exists among these workers (and is presented in this volume) regarding the appropriateness of extending the notion of role taking to cover all forms of social understanding. Without directly addressing this issue, I shall summarize in the final section all studies investigating the variety of general social conceptions that Mead might have subsumed under the notion of generalized role taking, and leave to the reader the task of evaluating the relation between these findings and the role-taking concept.

## emergence of the role-taking act

There are a number of methods that have been used to assess the emergence of the act of role taking. Flavell (1968) reports a series of studies in which children's role taking was assessed by presenting children with games or tasks in which taking the role of the other was necessary for successful performance. Feffer (1959, 1970) and Feffer and Gourevitch (1960) used a procedure that required children to change and coordinate perspectives by telling and retelling a story from the perspectives of different characters. Selman (1971) and Selman and Byrne (1974) have presented children with hypothetical stories about events in the lives of children and probed subjects for understanding and explanation of the actions and feelings of the characters.

Results from all these studies are presented in the form of stagelike levels of role taking, each level formally describing the relation attained between self's and other's perspectives. In general, these levels are framed according to the degree to which the self's and the other's subjectivity is recognized and the degree to which the implications of this recognition for mutual understanding are realized. The earliest stage in all of the systems involves a lack of acknowledgement of the other's subjectivity. The next stage involves recognition of the subjectivity of the other but with little ability to see the implications of this or to specify how one understands a subjective other. Later stages reveal the development of fuller understanding of subjectivity. Feffer's levels are described in terms of how differentiation of internal subjective states from external observable behaviors makes possible an increasing coordination of the actions and feeling of people as when a fictional social interaction is viewed from the perspective of each character. Flavell's levels are framed as an account of how the child recognizes that the other is also a "taker of roles" and of how he or she develops the implications of this interpersonal understanding. Selman's levels focus on how the child's recognition of subjectivity in the other brings a child to the realization that role taking is an inferential process, and on how this realization is followed by increasing sophistication in the kinds of evidence that a child uses to infer the internal state of another.

Hoffman (1975, 1977) has proposed a general framework for viewing role taking as a process of orienting toward others. He suggests that what is traditionally termed "role taking" should be subsumed under a larger developmental process of acquiring a cognitive sense of the other. Hoffman points to a growing body of evidence that children at very young ages are able to perform tasks that require some understanding of the thoughts of others, provided that these tasks are simple enough in content and that the form of response used to assess this understanding is behavioral. Four periods in the development of a cognitive sense of the other are proposed: (1) early fusion between self and other, (2) initial recognition of other's continued existence at about ten to twelve months of age, (3) development later in infancy of a rudimentary sense that the other has independent inner states, with elaborations of this notion (as in the accounts of Feffer, Flavell, and Selman) through childhood and into adolescence, and (4) awareness by middle or late childhood that others have personal histories and general life circumstances that contribute to their inner states of the moment.

### taking the role of persons-in-contexts

Investigation of the development of skills needed to take the role of the other during an actual interaction has also relied on several methods. In some, the problem is approached directly by asking children to communicate with another under special conditions (for example, a subject must describe a picture to another who is visually separated from the subject). Here the child's role-taking ability becomes evident through the nature of his or her communicative behavior. In others, children are presented with detailed accounts of hypothetical situations and of the behavior of persons in them. They are probed for role-taking ability as shown by their ability to recognize and synthesize information about behavior in relation to the context of these hypothetical situations.

Studies of children's referential communication ability have been summarized by Glucksberg, Krauss, and Higgins (1975). Evidence, in general, is as follows: (1) When children are simply exposed to the other's listener characteristics, prior to age six, they do not normally modify their messages to try to adapt to the listener's needs, (2) when children are explicitly informed of the listener's comprehension or non-comprehension of messages (that is, when they are given optimal feedback), accurate modification of messages (as measured by the other's comprehension) appears in children of age six, and (3) accurate modification regardless of feedback does not appear consistently until age nine or ten.

Shatz and Gelman (1973) examined the speech of four-year-old children to both age-mates and two-year-olds, looking for evidence of any modification (that is, not only accurate or adaptive modification), They found that listener age was significantly related to the mean length of utterance in their young subjects and argued that this constituted evidence of role taking earlier than had been previously documented. This finding, however, has been reinterpreted through a social learning model (Sherwood, 1977) and has been brought into question by a similar finding in which baby dolls rather than two-year-olds were used as listeners (Sachs and Devin, 1975).

Research on affective role taking has attempted to measure children's ability to take the role of persons-in-contexts in inferring emotions of others. Some evidence for very precocious abilities in this area (in children as young as three) has advanced, but these findings have drawn considerable criticism. Shantz (1975), for example, has suggested that such findings may really reflect egocentric projection of emotions in cases where accidental similarity between subjects and the hypothetical other produces seemingly accurate role taking. Children do not appear to take the role of others regarding emotional experiences when the other is unlike them or when the situation is outside their own personal experience until seven to nine years of age.

## taking the role of the usual person

The ability to predict the usual behavior of another in a future context, based on past information about the other's behavior, requires a means for the inference of behavioral tendencies and a general theory of context. The first of these abilities is the one that has received some study to date, although this work has been indirect. Rather than directly asking children to generate behavioral predictions about known others, investigators have collected data about children's descriptions of others and have looked within this data for the kinds of characterization that would form the basis for predictive capacity. Since the format in which the descriptions are usually obtained is open-ended (for example, beginning with the request to "tell me about your friend"), investigators have referred to this data as free description.

Findings from the major free description studies (Lively and Bromley, 1973; Peevers and Secord, 1973; Scarlett, Press and Crockett, 1971) are reviewed by Shantz (1975). Generally, these findings indicate: (1) the proportion of psychological descriptions of the other (that is, descriptions referring to covert psychological rather than overt physical or behavioral characteristics) increases significantly between the ages of seven and nine, (2) children younger than seven or eight tend to focus on static, concrete characterizations of the other (for example, appearance) or on globally evaluative traits like "nice" or "mean," while children older than eight include abstract characterizations (for example, characterization by reference to general behavioral patterns), (3) children older than eight make increasing use of interpersonal characterizations, which describe the other in terms of his or her effect on associates, and (4) by age ten to twelve, explicit qualification of characterizations of others begins to appear, including specification of how situational variables may interact with behavioral tendencies to produce behavior.

Some recent studies published since Shantz's review add to our base of information concerning children's ability to utilize notions of behavioral tendency in understanding others. Hendrick and others (1975) studied children five through eleven years of age to gauge their ability to combine trait pairs and evaluate how likeable a person would be who possessed a given combination of traits. All subjects in this sample appeared to use a simple additive strategy for evaluating the combination of traits, even in cases where these traits were contradictory (for example, friendly-terrible). This study suggests that the prediction of others' behavior may be very difficult in the many cases where the pertinent behavioral tendencies are in opposition to one another. Another form of conflict involving behavioral tendencies has been studied by Mapley (1976), who looked at children's tendency to distort the retelling of filmed episodes where persons in "good" roles (such as, doctor) were depicted doing "bad" actions (such as shoplifting) and vice versa. Mapley found that young children tended to distort the retelling so that the behavioral tendencies associated with persons in certain roles were not in conflict with the filmed episode.

*Constructing the Generalized Other.* As mentioned in the introduction, the research that which might be viewed by Mead as relevant to understanding of a generalized other has taken a variety of forms. A variety of agendas have guided such research; often the desire of the investigator is to map an area of social understanding for its own sake, without any consideration of how such understanding might contribute to role taking. Below, we review findings in three areas, each of which might be construed as documenting the construction of understanding regarding a generalized other or society in general. The import of these findings for the explication of role-taking development per se is left open.

*Universal Characteristics of Persons.* The study of universal properties of persons has proceeded farthest in studies of intentionality—the idea that all persons engage in planning before they act. The child's growing understanding of others' intentions was first investigated by Piaget (1965) in his work on children's moral evaluations of others' actions. In this research, Piaget suggests that children up to age eight or nine consider primarily the outcome of an action in determining blame, and only after nine does the actor's prior intention become a factor in blame evaluation.

A variety of investigators have attempted to reexamine the experimental situations used by Piaget. These students have isolated the effects of several variables and somewhat modified Piaget's original finding. Shantz (1975) summarizes much of this research. The findings, in general, are as follows: (1) unless the outcome of an action is very extreme, children do make differential moral evaluations of intended and unintended behavior as early as age six, thus distinguishing intended from unintended behavior at an earlier age than Piaget implied, and (2) extension of the intended/unintended distinction into more complex forms continues through childhood and into adolescence. For example, distinctions between intentional misdeed and simple carelessness are not made until middle childhood, and the understanding of insanity as an impairment of intentional ability does not exist until early adolescence. Since the time of Shantz's review, Berndt and Berndt (1975) have studied children's understanding of motive for behavior, differentiating near (immediate) behavioral motives from far (more distant) motives; for example, a child may injure another to obtain a toy (near motive) that he or she wants to use in an activity (far motive). In a condition where children were shown filmed episodes of behavior, Berndt and Berndt (1975) find that the understanding of both preschool and young elementary school children is better for near motives than for far motives. The investigators suggest that judgements of intentionality may involve complex considerations of motives of both types, and that understanding of motives themselves may precede facility with intentional judgements that require complex motivational considerations.

Related to intentions and motives is the notion of psychological causality. Research in this area has focused on how children explain the relation between persons' internal states and their external behavior. Studies of this type usually present subjects with some sample of individual behavior and ask for explanations of why the individual might have performed the depicted behavior. Of particular interest in this line of research is children's understanding of multiple or interactional causes of behavior. This form of causal explanation is one that appears most directly applicable to human behavior (Bunge, 1959) and has been identified as prominent among the actual causal explanations of behavior made by adults (Kelley, 1973). Multiple causality has been studied in children's direct explanation of behavior (Smith, 1976; Forbes, 1976), in children's determination of when a behavior is "kind" (Baldwin and Baldwin, 1970), in children's understanding of psychological defense mechanisms (Whiteman, 1967), and in children's judgements about reasons for succeeding or failing (Shultz and others, 1975). Generally these findings have been consistent: Children younger than about age nine are not capable of understanding multiple causality. However, some possibly contradictory findings exist. Lepper, Greene, and Nisbet (1973) found what might be interpreted as an unconscious operation of multiple causality in preschool children's self-attributions during a drawing task. Shultz and Butowsky (1977), concurring with Lepper, suggest that the abstractness of behavioral accounts used for stimulus materials in past studies may serve to mask the child's comprehension of multiple causality. In their own study, Shultz and Butowsky presented children with filmed accounts of behavior, and in this condition almost all of their preschool subjects were able to demonstrate multiple causal understanding by spontaneously mentioning both internal and external causes for behavior.

*Social Roles and Relations.* The study of children's understanding regarding the roles that one may occupy in society and the relations that exist between persons has also been a focus of some study. As yet, most of the work has been on social relations rather than roles, and most of this work has focused on one type of relation—friendship.

Selman has described four levels in children's conceptions of friendship. His work is summarized elsewhere in this volume. Damon (1977), synthesizing Selman's friendship levels with similar ones described by Youniss (1975, this volume) derived three basic levels of friendship conception in children ages four through thirteen. Level 1 conceptions define friendship in terms of frequent contact with another or in terms of the other's direct actions (such as sharing or playing). At level 2, friendship is a relation that is reciprocally valuable to both parties and is exemplified in the mutual response of two parties to each other's needs. Emphasis is now placed on the importance of trust. At the third and final level, friendship involves intentional maintenance of various psychological intimacies (like secrets).

Bigelow (1977) reports a study of children's friendship conceptions between the ages of six and fourteen. Nine dimensions of friendship relation were extracted by a cluster analysis of free description material on "what you want your best friend to be like." These dimensions were labeled: (1) common activities, (2) evaluation of other, (3) propinquity, (4) admiration, (5) acceptance, (6) loyalty and commitment, (7) genuineness, (8) common interests, and (9) intimacy potential.

Three stages in the development of friendship emerged, in substantial agreement with previous findings. The first level defines friendships as common activity, positive evaluation, and propinquity. The second level adds the notion of admiration (an ongoing positive attitude toward the other). At the third level, friendship includes acceptance, loyalty and commitment, genuineness, common interests, and potential for intimacy. Beyond friendship, there has been little study of children's understanding of social relations other than Damon's (1977) research on children's authority conceptions and related work in the moral-development tradition, which is beyond the scope of this brief review.

There is one rather interesting study of children's conceptions of social roles that should be reported. Garvey and Berndt (1975) examined the nature of roles as they were spontaneously portrayed by children in fantasy play. Her subjects were divided into three age groups: children aged thirty-four to thirty-nine months, forty-five to fifty-two months, and fifty-five to sixty-seven months. Examining the structure of role playing in her subjects' fantasy play, Garvey noted the construction of role relations with which the children were personally familiar (for example, mother-baby) in even the youngest subjects. Subjects in the oldest group were able to construct fantasy role relations that they could only have observed (for example, husband-wife) and were able to coordinate these roles over series of pretend interactions (for example, fixing the car or taking a trip). From Garvey's evidence, it appears that children begin to develop rudimentary understanding of the behavioral patterns associated with some roles as early as three, and are already displaying some facility in elaboration of role-consent behavioral patterns as early as four and one-half.

*Social Regulatons and Institutions.* Children's understanding of the institutions that emerge from collective social action and the needs of society at large, and of social conventions or norms that serve to regulate behavior into socially consensual forms, has been to object of considerable study. The work of Turiel (1975, 1978, this volume) or understanding of social conventionality and social structure and the work of Furth (1976, this volume) on understanding institutions such as school and institutional phenomena such as money are presented elsewhere in this volume.

In addition to the interview studies of Turiel and Furth, Coie and Pennington (1976) have presented a study of children's usage of the idea of deviance in a task of simple judgement. Children were presented with hypothetical stories about actors who were engaged in deviant actions (for example, getting into fights for no apparent reason or thinking that other children are "out to get them") and were asked after the story to judge the degree of similarity between the actor in the story and most children. Then they were asked to offer explanations for the behavior of the actors in the story. Results indicated that first grade children failed to see deviance in the stories and did not rate actors in the deviance stories as significantly different from most children. More interestingly, when asked to explain the actors' behavior, first grade subjects reconstructed the events in the story so that the actors were less deviant, rationalizing the actions and distorting the facts of the story. These results suggest that young children are not prepared to recognize that unusual events actually happen—a finding that conforms to Turiel's description of social-conventional understanding in young children.

## general commentary and conclusions

In a recent review of the relation between perspective-taking and moral development, Kurdek (1978) reports a consistent lack of convergent validity in the variety of measures that have been used to assess perspective taking. Correlations of measures used to assess different aspects of this ability (which Kurdek classifies into "spatial," "cognitive," and "affective" role-taking tasks) have been low or non-significant, as have been correlations between tasks that purportedly measure the same aspect. Kurdek's review suggests that before a complex issue such as the relation between role taking and moral development is raised, considerable effort must be expended in the explication of what the requisite cognitive abilities and conceptual understandings are within the area of role taking. In her review of the relation between social cognition and social behavior. Shantz (1975) concludes that a more coherent picture of this relation would be obtained if a variety of facets of both behavior and cognition were assessed and the relations between and within these domains were analyzed. Turiel (forthcoming, this volume) has suggested that role taking should be distinguished from social cognition entirely. He suggests that role taking should be viewed as an information-gathering ability, whose maturation is less qualitative than quantitative. It also should be distinguished from social-conceptual development, whose maturation is more qualitatively developmental in the structuralist sense.

All of these authors appear to be making a point, which should be underscored in a general commentary on the literature of social cognition. The field has become a rather diverse one. It has certainly come a long way since Flavell lamented in 1968 that "just what sorts of beginning role-taking skills (or precursors thereof) may develop during early childhood is still a question for which no previous research provides an answer" (p. 26). Through diversity, however, one may produce either comprehensive synthesis or diffuseness and ambiguity. As Kurdek, Shantz, and Turiel seem to suggest, the time has come for a decisive move toward the former of these alternatives. Piaget certainly pointed the lead in this direction nearly fifty years ago when he began his studies of children's intellectual development, armed with categorical distinctions drawn from the work of epistemologists. He continues to point to the importance of this consideration through his more recent reliance on concepts of propositional logic.

The value of a priori analysis has as yet, however, received short shrift among researchers in social cognition. In the most extreme cases, studies have examined children's role taking with the seeming assumption that role taking is what the role-taking task tests. This trend cannot continue if our understanding of children is to develop in as orderly a fashion as we suspect their understanding of the social world develops.

Turiel's distinction between skills of information gathering and structures for conceptual understanding (or information processing) seems a good one. His procedure of a priori logical analysis within the latter domain, with subsequent empirical validation of categories, exemplifies a procedure of investigation that has the promise of producing synthesis of findings within an integrative general theory. The need exists for further efforts in this direction. We must develop alternative analyses of the structure of social conception that attempt to integrate past findings and to generate future research. Certainly, we require also an analysis of the informational skills involved in social understanding in order to complement any analysis of the informational skills involved in social understanding in order to complement any analysis of conceptual structure. Diverse research regarding children's understanding of the social import of language, paralinguistic behavior, and nonverbal communication must be integrated into findings from social cognition. Studies of children's capacities for identifying and categorizing social contexts must also be undertaken.

The relation between cognitive skills and real-life behavior in children, an issue of considerable contemporary interest, will of necessity await progress in these areas. When one is faced with a domain of action that is almost certainly regulated through the complex interplay of a wide array of cognitive skills, little hope exists for a real understanding of how the former comes under control of the latter unless the complexity of the latter is reasonably well understood.

## suggested readings

The following sources were invaluable in the preparation of this review and should prove to be of considerable value to those who are interested in pursuing the literature on children's social cognition.

Damon, W. *The Social World of the Child.* San Francisco: Jossey-Bass, 1977. This book reports some of the most comprehensive studies to date on children's understanding of social interactions, social relations, and social institutions and regulations.

Glucksberg, S., Krauss, R. M., and Higgins, T. "The Development of Referential Communication Skills." In F. Horowitz (Ed.), *Review of Child Development Research.* Vol. 4. Chicago: University of Chicago Press, 1975. This review of literature on children's communication skills is the most recent and integrative of efforts in this area.

Hoffman, M. L. "Personality and Social Development." *Annual Review of Psychology,* 1977, *28,* 295-321. This is an excellent review of more recent research, including sex-role development, moral internalization, and intrinsic motivation.

Kurdek, L. "Perspective Taking as the Cognitive Basis of Children's Moral Development: A Review of the Literature." *Merrill-Palmer Quarterly,* 1978, *24,* 3-28. This article summarizes an extensive number of research efforts aimed at explicating the nature of social cognition and its relations to moral reasoning and behavior. It succinctly points out the reasons for ambiguity in these areas.

Lively, W., and Bromley, D. *Person Perception in Childhood and Adolescence.* London: Wiley, 1973. Nearly all of the research on children's free descriptions of others is either replicated or presented for the first time in this ambitious empirical effort.

Mischel, T. *Understanding Other Persons.* Totowa, N. J.: Rowman and Littlefield, 1974. This book contains a series of scholarly psychological and philosophical essays on the problem of social understanding and regulation of social behavior.

Rosenberg, S., and Sedlak, A. "Structural Representations in Implicit Personality Theory." In L. Berkowitz (Ed.), *Advances in Experimental and Social Psychology.* Vol. 6. New York: Academic Press, 1972. This article presents important theoretical and methodological issues in the study of people's systems for characterizing others.

Shantz, C. U. "The Development of Social Cognition." In E. M. Hetherington (Ed.), *Review of Child Development Research.* Chicago: University of Chicago Press, 1975. This article is a comprehensive review of material published prior to 1975.

**138**

## references

Baldwin, C. P. and Baldwin, A. L. "Children's Judgments of Kindness." *Child Development*. 1970, *41*, 29-47.

Baldwin, J. M. *Social and Ethical Interpretations of Mental Development*. New York: Macmillan, 1906.

Berndt, T. J., and Berndt, E. G. "Children's Use of Motives and Intentionality in Person Perception and Moral Judgement." *Child Development*, 1975, *46*, 904-912.

Bigelow, B. "Children's Friendship Expectations: A Cognitive-Developmental Study." *Child Development*, 1977, *48*, 246-253.

Bunge, M. *Causality: The Place of the Causal Principle in Modern Science*. Cambridge, Mass.: Harvard University Press, 1959.

Coie, J. and Pennington, B. "Children's Perceptions of Deviance and Disorder." *Child Development*, 1976, *47*, 407-413.

Damon, W. *The Social World of the Child*. San Francisco: Jossey-Bass, 1977.

Feffer, M. "Developmental Analysis of Interpersonal Behavior." *Psychological Review*, 1970, *77*, 197-214.

Feffer, M. "The Cognitive Implications of Role-Taking Behavior." *Journal of Personality*, 1960, *28*, 383-396.

Feffer, M., and Gourevitch, V. "Cognitive Aspects of Role-Taking in Children." *Journal of Personality*, 1960, *28*, 383-396.

Flavell, J. H. *The Development of Role-Taking and Communication Skills in Children*. New York: Wiley, 1968.

Forbes, D. "The Development of Psychological Causality." Unpublished master's thesis, Clark University, 1976.

Furth, H. "Children's Conception of Social Institutions: A Piagetian Framework." *Human Development*, 1976, *19* (6), 351-374.

Gage, N. L., and Cronbach, L. J. "Conceptual and Methodological Problems in Interpersonal Perception." *Psychological Review*, 1955, *62*, 411-422.

Garvey, C., and Berndt, R. "The Organization of Pretend Play." Unpublished manuscript, Johns Hopkins University, 1975.

Glucksberg, S., Krauss, R. M., and Higgins, T. "The Development of Referential Communication Skills." In F. Horowitz (Ed.), *Review of Child Development Research*. Vol. 4. Chicago: University of Chicago Press, 1975.

Hendrick, C., Franz, C. M., and Hoving, K. L. "How Do Children Form Impressions of Persons?" *Memory and Cognition*, 1975, *3*, 325-328.

Hoffman, M. L. "Personality and Social Development." *Annual Review of Psychology*, 1977, *28*, 259-321.

Hoffman, M. L. "Developmental Synthesis of Affect and Cognition and Its Implications for Altruistic Motivation." *Developmental Psychology*, 1975, *11*, 607-622.

Inhelder, B., and Piaget, J. *The Growth of Logical Thinking from Childhood to Adolescence*. New York: Basic Books, 1958.

Kelley, H. H. "The Process of Causal Attribution. *American Psychologist*, 1973, *28*, 107-128.

Kurdek, L. "Perspective Taking as the Cognitive Basis of Children's Moral Development: A Review of the Literature." *Merrill-Palmer Quarterly*, 1978, *24*, 3-28.

Lepper, M., Greene, D., and Nisbet, R. "Undermining Children's Intrinsic Interest with Extrinsic Reward: A Test of the Overjustification Hypothesis." *Journal of Personality and Social Psychology*, 1973, *28*, 129-137.

Lively, W. J., and Bromley, D. B. *Person Perception in Childhood and Adolescence*. London: Wiley, 1973.

Mapley, G. "Cognitive Complexity as an Explanation of Children's Distortion of Filmed

Episodes of Incongruous Interpersonal Behavior." Unpublished doctoral dissertation, Wayne State University, 1976.

Mead, G. H. *Mind, Self, and Society.* Chicago: University of Chicago Press, 1934.

Peevers, B. H., and Secord, P. F. "Developmental Changes in Attribution of Descriptive Concepts to Persons." *Journal of Personality and Social Psychology,* 1973, *27,* 120-128.

Piaget, J. *The Moral Judgment of the Child.* New York: Free Press, 1965.

Sachs, J., and Devin, J. "Young Children's Use of Age Appropriate Speech Styles in Social Interaction and Role Playing." *Journal of Child Language,* 1975, *3,* 81-98.

Scarlett, H. H., Press, A. N., and Crockett, W. H. "Children's Descriptions of Peers: A Wernerian Developmental Analysis." *Child Development,* 1971, *42,* 439-454.

Selman, R. "Taking Another's Perspective: Role-Taking in Early Childhood." *Child Development,* 1971, *42,* 1721-1734.

Selman, R., and Byrne, D. F. "A Structural-Developmental Analysis of Levels of Role-Taking in Middle Childhood." *Child Development,* 1974, *45,* 803-806.

Shantz, C. U. "The Development of Social Cognition." In E. M. Hetherington (Ed.), *Review of Child Development Research.* Vol. 5. Chicago: University of Chicago Press 1975.

Shatz, M., and Gelman, R. "The Development of Communication Skills: Modification in the Speech of Young Children as a Function of Listener." *Monographs of the Society for Research in Child Development,* 1973, *38,* 1-38.

Shaw, M., and Sulzer, J. "An Empirical Test of Heider's Levels in Attribution of Responsibility." *Journal of Abnormal and Social Psychology,* 1964, *69,* 39-46.

Sherwood, V. "Age Related Change on Non-Verbal Communication: Indices of Comprehension/Non-Comprehension in Child Listeners." Unpublished master's thesis, Clark University, 1977.

Shultz, T., and Butowsky, I. "Young Children's Use of the Scheme of Multiple Sufficient Causality in Real vs. Hypothetical Situations." *Child Development,* 1977, *48,* 464-470.

Shultz, T., and others. "Development of Schemes for the Attribution of Multiple Psychological Causes." *Developmental Psychology,* 1975, *11,* 502-510.

Smith, M. "Children's Use of the Multiple Sufficient Cause Schema in Social Perception." *Journal of Personality and Social Psychology,* 1976, *32,* 737-747.

Turiel, E. "The Development of Concepts of Social Structure." In J. Glick and A. Clarke-Stewart (Eds.), *Studies in Social and Cognitive Development.* Vol. 1. New York: Gardner Press, 1978.

Turiel, E. "The Development of Social Concepts: Mores, Customs, and Conventions." In D. J. DePalma and F. M. Foley (Eds.), *Moral Development: Current Theory and Research.* Hillsdale, N.J.: L. Erlbaum, 1975.

Whiteman, M. "Children's Conceptions of Psychological Causality." *Child Development,* 1967, *38,* 143-155.

Youniss, J. "Another Perspective on Social Cognition." In A. Pick (Ed.), *Minnesota Symposium on Child Psychology.* Vol. 9. Minneapolis: University of Minnesota Press, 1975.

*David Forbes is a graduate student in psychology at Clark University, Worcester, Massachusetts.*

# index